GW00383861

KUWAIT

KUWAIT

Vanguard of the Gulf

PETER MANSFIELD

Hutchinson

LONDON   SYDNEY   AUCKLAND

JOHANNESBURG

Hutchinson Publishing Co Ltd

An imprint of the Random Century Group
20 Vauxhall Bridge Road, London SW1V 2SA

Random Century Australia (Pty) Ltd
20 Alfred Street, Milsons Point, Sydney, NSW 2061

Random Century New Zealand Limited
191 Archers Road, PO Box 40–086, Glenfield, Auckland 10

Century Hutchinson South Africa (Pty) Ltd
PO Box 337, Bergvlei 2012, South Africa

First published 1990

Set in Photina by Vision Typesetting, Manchester

Printed and bound in Great Britain by Mackays of Chatham, Chatham, Kent

British Library Cataloguing in Publication Data
Mansfield, Peter
Kuwait: vanguard of the Gulf.
1. Kuwait. Social conditions
I. Title
953′.67053

ISBN 0 09 1736048

Contents

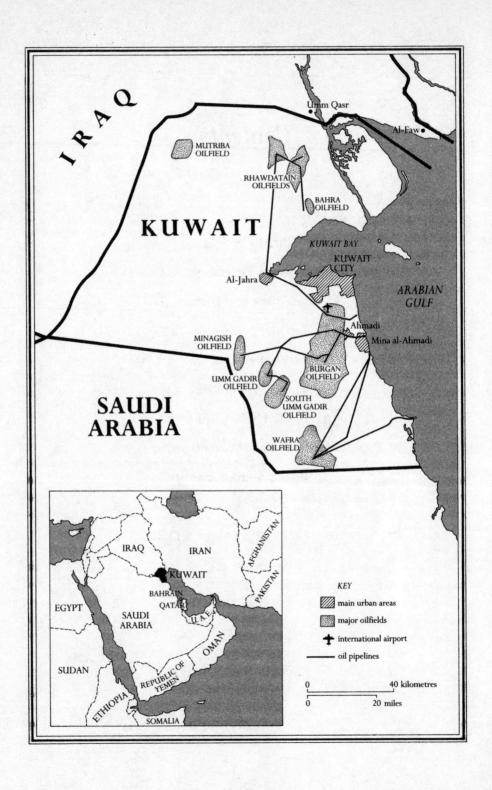

Introduction

In 1961, when I was editing the *Middle East Forum*, a monthly magazine published by the Alumni Association of the American University of Beirut, I made an extended visit to Kuwait. It was not the first time I had been there. That was early in 1958, when the little desert emirate was only just beginning to attract international attention as the first of the kind to become vastly wealthy from its oil. The old mud walls of the city had recently been pulled down and the first and only modern multi-storied building had been constructed opposite the Jahra Gate, which had been left standing as a symbol of the past.

Three years later the situation was different. Kuwait was about to attain full independence through the ending of the sixty-two-year-old special relationship with Britain. The state of Kuwait would be able to join both the Arab League and the United Nations and conduct its own diplomacy as well as manage its internal affairs as it had done for two centuries. At the same time it had become apparent that the generally prudent use of Kuwait's wealth under the supervision of its exceptionally wise ruler, Shaikh Abdallah Salem al-Sabah, was producing a remarkable transformation of Kuwaiti society. The abolition of poverty and illiteracy among Kuwait's citizens was a clearly attainable objective.

I returned to Beirut feeling enthusiastic. It was not simply that Kuwait was demonstrating a unique kind of laboratory experiment in the rapid improvement of living standards of an impoverished society. The results were already fascinating and one had to admit that the obvious potential for disaster only made the situation more interesting. The real reason for my excitement was that I could foresee, although still only dimly, a very special role for Kuwait in the Arab renaissance that was taking place. Obviously there was no question of Kuwait being a 'big power' among the Arabs such as Egypt, Syria and Iraq or as Saudi Arabia would surely become. But, as a centre of learning, research and expertise, it had a rare opportunity. That it would become a major financial centre was already clear. It would be able to gain experience in the investment of reserves, in establishing a range of financial institutions and organizing the flow of aid to Arab and other Third World countries.

In 1961 the idea of establishing in Kuwait the first university in the Arab Gulf states, with all its implications for the region, was being discussed. Why not also set up a centre for scientific research to concentrate on the special problems and opportunities of Arabia: desert agriculture, sea-water desalination and solar energy? (Marine pollution was not high on the agenda in those days.) Perhaps Kuwait could establish the first copyright library in the Arab world. Then there was the task of translation. It was not fanciful to consider the possibility of Kuwait sponsoring a huge programme to make available to the Arab-speaking world the most important achievements in science and literature of other cultures. In this it would merely be following the example of Baghdad under the Abbasids of the eighth century – which saw the translation of the major works of science and philosophy of the Hellenistic and Indian civilizations.

My idealistic musings along these lines at a Beirut dinner party met with a startling reaction from an old friend, a scion of one of the grand Sunni Lebanese political families. How could I talk such rubbish, he demanded. Everybody knew that Kuwait was a purely artificial creation to serve the interests of the British. It was an absurdity, with no *raison d'être*. Its resources belonged to all the Arabs and should be distributed among them.

In vain I tried to persuade my outraged friend to consider the matter in a strictly practical manner. I asked him to consider the alternative to an independent State of Kuwait. Should it be part of Iraq (as the slightly deranged Iraqi leader Abdul Karim Kassem was shortly to declare that it was)? My friend clearly did not think so. Should it have been absorbed into the kingdom of Saudi Arabia in the 1930s or into Gamal Abdul Nasser's United Arab Republic of the 1950s? Although marginally more sympathetic to both these propositions, my friend still found them irrelevant. What mattered to him was that Kuwait was merely one more of the artificial nation states that the European powers had carved out of the Arab world for their own benefit.

I believe that the experience of the past twenty years has proved my optimism to have been valid. Few Kuwaitis would claim that all the hopes that they or their parents placed in their country at the time of independence have been fulfilled. Indeed, some of them are markedly critical of the domestic, social and economic policies and the foreign policies that have been pursued. Most agree, however, that Kuwait has overwhelmingly justified its existence as an independent state in the ways that suggested themselves to me in the early months of 1961.

But how far was my Lebanese friend correct in suggesting that the very concept of an independent Kuwait was a British invention?

He was indisputably correct in saying that for more than a century Britain had wanted to prevent Kuwait either from coming under the influence of a rival power or from being swallowed up entirely by a larger state. At first the threats had come from other European countries – France, Germany or Russia – or the Ottoman empire, and it was to guard against such threats that the Exclusive Agreement between Britain and Kuwait was signed in 1899. In more recent times Britain had grown concerned that Kuwait might be absorbed by another Middle Eastern state – Iraq, Iran or Saudi Arabia – or, what seemed much worse to those British who were in a state of post-Suez paranoia, that Kuwait might become part of a pan-Arab unity led by Nasser's Egypt. As Kuwait had become a major oil producer, successive British governments had come to regard it as a vital interest. Those were the days when it still seemed inconceivable that Britain should ever abandon the Gulf. The present generation, to whom imperial pretensions are hardly even a memory, may need reminding that Britain's decision to withdraw was made in a sudden and unexpected *volte face* by the Wilson government in 1968. I recall a very senior British official in the Middle East saying to me as late as 1965 that there was no question of any British Parliament 'ever' agreeing to the withdrawal of the British military base from Aden. For him the logic was quite simple. The main function of the Aden base was to protect the oil of the Gulf and especially that of Kuwait. Kuwaiti oil was after all the main pillar of sterling.

Although my Lebanese friend would have felt that such a view gave weight to his own opinion of Kuwait, it by no means proves that Kuwait was a British invention – even if some of the British had come to believe that it was. One of the troubles for the Western, and especially the British, reader is that nearly all the standard works of reference in English quite understandably see Kuwait through Western eyes. This is true of J.G. Lorimer's magisterial *Gazetteer of the Persian Gulf, Oman and Central Arabia*, originally published in 1908 in six volumes, as it is of the memoirs of officials who served in the region and the reports of passing travellers. Many of these writings demonstrate great erudition and sympathy but they do not convey much feeling of how the Kuwaitis see themselves and their own past. Perhaps one rare exception is the Lebanese American writer and traveller Amin Rihani, who visited Kuwait in the early 1920s. A Maronite born in Mount Lebanon, he was an American citizen who was exceptionally at home in two cultures. But some of his many writings are unavailable in English, including what is probably his best-known work in the Arab world, *Muluk al-Arab* (*Kings of the Arabs*), which has a chapter on the ruling Sabah family of Kuwait.

When I visited Kuwait in 1979 a young British diplomat, who was under the impression that I was on my first visit to the region, told me, 'I find that the best way to explain Kuwaiti society to visitors is to say that if you scratch an educated Kuwaiti you will find under his *dishdasha* a British public schoolboy.' Another, rather less ludicrous, opinion is that Kuwait's experiment in constitutional government after independence was made entirely on British advice. Not unnaturally Kuwaitis reject this view of themselves; indeed some claim the British connection was either merely harmful or of no importance at all. After all, if you feel, as Kuwaitis do, that you are heirs to an ancient culture and a religion which completes and perfects the other monotheistic faiths, the 'British episode' in your history is likely to dwindle in significance. But with very few exceptions* the writings by Kuwaitis about their own society and history appear only in Arabic. This book is a modest attempt by a Briton who has known Kuwait for three decades to synthesize the Western and Kuwaiti view of this remarkable little state.

---

*One of these is Muhammad Rumaihi's *Beyond Oil: Unity and Development in the Gulf*, al-Saqi, 1986.

I

The Predecessors

The word 'Kuwait' is the Arabic diminutive of *kut*, which means a castle or fort and is a common place-name in the region. Normally a *kut* lies near the sea or a river. Kut al-Amara on the Euphrates was the site of a painful British surrender to the Turks in the First World War. A close look at a map of the Middle East shows why Kuwait's importance has depended not only on the discovery of oil.

The town of Kuwait, which is the capital of the present state, lies on the southern shore of a great sweeping bay which is situated at the north-western end of the Arabian Gulf. This provides a superb harbour, which an official from the Bombay government described in 1845 as capable of containing the entire British navy.

Kuwait is the principal outlet to the ocean of the Great Arabian Desert, which stretches from Najd, the central plateau of the Peninsula. To thirsty travellers in the past it was affectionately known as 'Najd by the Sea'. A few miles to the north-east, the Shatt al-Arab, formed by the confluence of the Tigris and Euphrates, flows into the Gulf.

No one knows exactly when the town of Kuwait was built, but it was some time early in the eighteenth century. The founders were the Utub, a clan of the Aniza tribe of nomads from Najd. A long series of droughts in the early eighteenth century drove the Anizas from Najd eastwards and northwards to the shores of the Gulf. This was part of a general movement of the Arab inhabitants of the Peninsula from southern Arabia, which was relatively fertile but could feed only a limited population, towards the Euphrates basin of Mesopotamia, and gave rise to the ancient Arab saying: 'Yemen is the cradle of the Arab, and Iraq is his grave.'

Some of the Utub, presumably after learning seafaring on the coast, set sail from Qatar and landed at Kuwait, which was then virtually uninhabited and consisted of little more than a small empty fortress

('Kuwait') belonging to the powerful Bani Khalid tribe, which then dominated the north-western region of the Gulf between Kuwait and Qatar. The new arrivals secured the protection of the Bani Khalid and set about building their town. It was after the death in 1752 of the ruler of the Bani Khalid, Shaikh Sulaiman bin Muhammad, that the Sabah family emerged at the head of the new settlement and the rulers of an independent shaikdom. According to strong tradition, the first Amir of Kuwait, Shaikh Sabah bin Jaber bin Adhbi, was chosen by the inhabitants to administer the affairs of the town and conduct justice. The present ruling family of Kuwait are his descendants.

Shortly afterwards another branch of the Utub – the Al Khalifa – became the rulers of Bahrain; they have remained so for two centuries. But while Kuwaitis and Bahrainis may consider the national entities to which they belong to be two hundred years old, they are increasingly conscious of the fact that the land they inhabit has a much more ancient history.

Over four thousand years ago, the Sumerians of Mesopotamia were trading through the Gulf, which they called the Bitter Sea or the Sea of the Rising Sun. In the Indus Valley, a thousand miles to the east, another great Bronze Age civilization was flourishing. About a century ago archaeologists began to suspect that between these two there had been a third civilization which was now lost; this is known as Dilmun. The first recorded reference to Dilmun was on one of the tablets dug up at Ur which belonged to the king of Lagash, who lived circa 2500 BC: 'The ships of Dilmun . . . brought me wood as tribute.' Subsequent excavations, which are still continuing, have confirmed early suspicions that Dilmun was focused on the Gulf and that Bahrain was its main trading centre; it was a vital link in the flow of metals, precious stones and ivory between India and Mesopotamia, and itself an exporter of wool and skins.

However, the Dilmun civilization extended far beyond Bahrain. The Danish archaeological team which made the crucial discoveries in Bahrain in the early 1950s went on to dig in Failaka Island, the eight-mile-long strip of land which stands at the entrance to Kuwait Bay. It found plentiful evidence from the pottery fragments and steatite seals that Failaka was the northern outpost of Dilmun and a flourishing community in its own right during the third millennium BC. This was not all that the Danes discovered. In the southern corners of Failaka they revealed a Greek temple, a factory to make terracotta statues and the outlines of a square-shaped town which proved to be a fortified outpost of the Seleucid empire, which succeeded Alexander the Great. Among a hoard of silver coins found near the temple was one which bore the head of the Syrian King Antiochus III, who ruled over the Seleucid empire from 223 to 187 BC. A rectangular slab of stone discovered near the hoard of coins carries a long inscription expressing 'the King's concern with the Island of Ikaros'.

This identification of Failaka with Ikaros is of great interest. Alexander himself never passed by Kuwait, although many Kuwaitis would like to believe that he did. When he reached the eastern limits of his eastern conquests in India in 326 BC, he set out to return to Persia by land. But he had in mind a great sea-traffic between Babylon, the capital of his eastern empire, and India. So he ordered his admiral Nearchus to return to the Euphrates via the Gulf at the head of his huge fleet. Nearchus kept a detailed journal of the journey which has not survived, but in 170 AD the Roman historian Arrian provided a full abstract of the work in his book on India. From this we know that Nearchus informed Alexander of the existence of two small islands at the head of the Gulf. One of these had wild goats and antelope which were sacred to the Goddess Artemis, and Alexander ordered that it should be named Ikaros after the island in the Aegean Sea which it resembled. The other island was presumably the smaller Aula, which Nearchus described as being well wooded.

Shortly after Alexander a Greek fortress outpost was established on Failaka/Ikaros and seems to have lasted for about two hundred years. A visitor may wonder how the Greeks survived the loneliness and the heat of summer with only their faith in Artemis 'the Saviouress' to sustain them. But perhaps they would not have been particularly lonely. Alexander's dream of a single united empire did not survive his death but the flow of trade continued and no doubt some ships called at Ikaros.

The discovery of the Seleucid settlement still left a mystery concerning the thousand years after the fading of the Dilmun civilization at the end of the late Bronze Age in about 1300 BC. The search continues, with the enthusiastic participation of the Kuwait department of antiquities and the staff of the National Museum. In 1985 a French archaeological team uncovered evidence on al-Khazna Hill at the southern end of Failaka of an earlier Hellenistic settlement dating back to at least the seventh century BC. Gradually the gap is being closed.

Unfortunately the evidence of what happened in the Gulf in the subsequent centuries is extremely sketchy. Roman historians such as Strabo (born in 63 BC) and Pliny (born in AD 23), who wrote of the region, never visited it but relied on hearsay and the works of earlier Greek writers which have disappeared. But it was Eratosthenes of Cyrene (276–194 BC), quoted by Strabo, who made the first mention of the existence of oil in the Gulf region:

Asphaltus is found in great abundance in Babylonia. The liquid asphaltus, which is called naphtha, is found in Susiana . . . it is of singular nature. When it is brought near the fire, the fire catches it, and if a body smeared over with it is brought near the fire, it burns with a flame, which it is impossible to extinguish, except with a large quantity of water.

Posidonius, who was writing a century later, is also quoted by Strabo as distinguishing between white and black naphtha: 'White naphtha, which attracts flame, is liquid sulphur: the second or black naphtha is liquid asphaltus, and is burnt in lamps instead of oil.'

What we do learn from Pliny is that in the last years of the rule of the Ptolemies in Egypt and in the years of Roman power – that is, the beginning of the Christian era – while a very large amount of trade was carried on between the Mediterranean and India, it was mainly through the Red Sea. The trade routes through the Gulf fell into decline. After the death of Cleopatra, the last Ptolemaic ruler, Egypt became a province of the Roman empire. Enormous strides were made in the science of navigating the treacherous waters of the Red Sea and great fleets began to sail through it to India. The Romans did not reach the Gulf until about AD 116, when the Emperor Trajan arrived there with high ambitions. Gibbon is characteristically scathing:

The praises of Alexander, transmitted by a succession of poets and historians, had kindled a dangerous emulation in the mind of Trajan. Like him, the Roman emperor undertook an expedition against the nations of the East; but he lamented with a sigh that his advanced age scarcely left him any hopes of equalling the renown of the son of Philip. Yet the success of Trajan, however transient, was rapid and specious. The degenerate Parthians, broken by intestine discord, fled before his arms. He descended the river Tigris in triumph, from the mountains of Armenia to the Persian Gulf. He enjoyed the honour of being the first, as he was the last, of the Roman generals who ever navigated that remote sea. His fleets ravaged the coasts of Arabia, and Trajan vainly flattered himself that he was approaching the confines of India . . . But the death of Trajan soon clouded the splendid prospect.

It was only a century later that activity in the Gulf began to revive, with the rise of the Persian Sassanian empire, which entered into a prolonged struggle with Rome. On the southern shore of the Gulf, Arab mariners were also becoming increasingly adventurous. They had discovered the monsoon or trade wind known as the Hippalus, and this encouraged them to sail into deeper waters instead of hugging the coast. During the reign of the

Sassanian King Shapur I (AD 309–317) the Arabs from Bahrain and al-Hasa launched frequent raids against the opposite coast.

Arabs and Persians contested the waters of the Gulf. Little more than three centuries later both these peoples belonged to the new great empire of Islam.

2

The Arabs and Islam

The racial origins of the Arabs are highly obscure. The Arabs themselves have inherited a tradition that they come from two stocks – the Qahtanis and Adnanis. The former originated in the rain-fed highlands of southwestern Arabia and are descended from the patriarch Qahtan. The latter come from the north and centre of the Peninsula and are descended from the patriarch Adnan. Almost every Arab tribe claimed descent from one or the other. Of the two it is the southerners or Yemenis who now form half the population of Arabia and are called the 'true Arabs', and it is the sons of Adnan who are *Mustarib* or Arabized Arabs. Although today there is no obvious racial difference between those who call themselves Qahtanis and those who call themselves Adnanis, there are two recognizable racial types among the inhabitants of Arabia. The tall people with clean-cut hawk-like features come mainly from the north; while those in the south tend to be smaller with softer and more rounded features – in origin they are probably related to the Ethiopians. It is therefore ironic that it is the southerners who are considered the 'true Arabs', for it is the others who provide the popular image of the Arab and it was in central and northern Arabia that the classical Arabic tongue – the vehicle of Arab/Islamic civilization – developed.

The early history of the people of south Arabia is still being uncovered through the study of a rich variety of inscriptions in their lost languages which are closely related to Arabic. The land was fertile enough to support settled communities which developed into complex and sophisticated states. One of the first of these little kingdoms was that of Saba, which arose about a thousand years before Christ, and it was a Sabaean king who built the great Marib Dam in about 750 BC in present-day eastern Yemen, which lasted more than 1200 years until it was allowed to break down (and is only now being restored).

While the kingdoms of the settled peoples of south Arabia rose and fell, the inhabitants of the centre and north of the Arabian Peninsula were largely nomadic, as they had been since about 10,000 BC, when the domestication of animals first made this way of life possible. The successive waves of population who were forced into the wilderness because the irrigated lands in the south were too limited to support them also became nomadic, raising their flocks of sheep and goats and herds of camels, and moving from one short-lived pasture to another. Although there were some who settled around the oases, and on the coasts, where they survived from trading and fishing, it was the nomadic tribes with their distinct values and traditions who were dominant. Sometimes the sedentary people abandoned their settlements to return to the freedom of the desert.

While the limitless desert gave the nomads a sense of liberty and proud independence, the harsh realities of the vast and riverless Peninsula imposed its own harsh discipline. Survival depended on the solidarity and self-protection of the tribe and the system whereby the whole family, clan or tribe was held responsible for the actions of any one of them. There was no written code of laws; individual crimes were restrained by the fear of lasting vengeance. No such restraints, however, applied to communal acts of violence. Inter-tribal disputes might be settled by an arbiter, a wise authority on tribal customs, but meanwhile they were the excuse for a *ghazu*, or raid, aimed chiefly at seizing your opponents' camels, which for many centuries could be regarded as the national sport of the Arabs.

These nomadic Arabs were animists by religion, in that they worshipped trees, rocks or water springs. Over the years this developed into a polytheism – a belief in a variety of spirits who could be of either sex and were often based on a particular rock or shrine. The most famous of these was the shrine at the Kaaba in Mecca, where the great Black Stone (probably a meteorite) was a place of pilgrimage for centuries before it became central to the religion of Islam.

This was not a high culture which could be compared with its contemporaries in Byzantium and Persia but it had one matchless strength in its language and a supreme artistic achievement in its poetry. This was always recited aloud, as in the Homeric age of ancient Greece. The poet was the spokesman of the tribe who sang the praises of its heroes and leaders and poured scorn on its enemies. Enough has survived for us to appreciate that he sang magnificently. It is no surprise that love of language remains a form of Arab patriotism.

By the beginning of the sixth century of the Christian era the whole of Arabia was a conglomeration of petty autonomous states. They had no frontiers but were grouped around tribal confederations. While the people were fiercely independent and proud of their way of life, they were not isolated from outside influences. Through their contacts with the Byzantine and Abyssinian empires, which were Christian, and the Persian Zoroastrian empire, they began to acquire monotheistic ideas. In the north-east the Arab kingdom of Hira was allied with Persia, and in the north-west the kingdom of Hira was usually allied with the Persian empire's rival power Byzantium.

It was in Mecca, one of the largest settled and relatively affluent trading communities in western Arabia, that the prophet Muhammad was born in about AD 571 – a man whose genius and inspiration helped to transform the history of mankind, a fact which is acknowledged not only by the one-fifth of the human race who subscribe to the faith that he founded. This is no place for a description of the Islamic religion, but certain aspects of it and its history are highly relevant to the story of Kuwait, as they are to that of all the modern Arab states.

The first of these is that, while Muslims do not believe Muhammad to be divine – for Islam is the most fiercely monotheistic of faiths, adhering to the belief that 'there is no God but God' – they do regard him as the last of God's messengers, or the seal of the prophets, who include Moses and Jesus. They therefore hold that Islam is the ultimate faith which completes and perfects the two other heavenly religions – Judaism and Christianity. If mankind as a whole has not yet accepted this truth, it is due to the failings of the community of Muslim believers.

Another important fact is that, while Muslims believe in paradise and the soul's immortality, their faith is far from other-worldly. The prophet, unlike Jesus, was a political leader and organizer of genius, and in Islam there is no separation between religion and politics and no concept of a secular state. The Holy Quran, which for Muslims is the literal word of God, is the continuing inspiration for all Muslim thought and action but it is not a comprehensive code of law. Muslims therefore have looked also to the example of the prophet and his companions. Their words and deeds, known as their *sunnah* or habitual modes of thought and action, were collected in the *hadith*, or traditions of the prophet, which were handed down through a line of reliable witnesses. Together the Quran and the *sunnah* form the sources of the Islamic *shariah*. This is normally translated as Islamic law but it is much more than this. It is neither canonical law (Islam has no priesthood) nor secular law, because no such concept exists in Islam. It is rather a whole system of social morality, prescribing the ways in which man should live if he is to act according to God's will. If he contravenes the *shariah*, his offence is against God and not the state.

This is an ideal. Since the earliest times Arab and Muslim rulers have assumed secular powers to some degree, and none more so than those of today. But the ideal continues to have a powerful influence on the hearts and minds of all Muslims. It accounts for the potent force of Utopianism among the Arabs – the belief that, if they were to return to the ways of the prophet and his companions, the triumph of Islam in this world would be assured. In the West this is usually described as Islamic fundamentalism, but in a real sense all Muslim believers are fundamentalist because they know that the Holy Quran was God's final message to mankind. The triumph of the West in the last two or three centuries is seen by Muslims as an aberration of history.

It is hardly surprising that Arabs of today are still inspired to the point of obsession by the story of the first achievements of Islam. When the prophet died in AD 632, the new faith had been accepted through most of Arabia. In one generation he had welded the scattered and idolatrous tribes of the Peninsula into one nation worshipping a single, all-powerful but compassionate deity. What followed was even more astonishing. Under the prophet's first two successors, or caliphs, Abu Bakr and Omar, the little army of the faithful went on to challenge the two great empires of the Near East – Byzantium and Persia. Abu Bakr's chief marshal, Khalid ibn al-Walid, who was one of the greatest generals of all time, defeated the Persians in a battle at Kazima, which is now in Kuwaiti territory on the northern side of Kuwait Bay. He then turned his attention to Byzantine-controlled Syria, which he swiftly conquered. The caliph Omar overthrew the Persian Sassanid empire. The Arab armies swept on into Egypt, which was a Byzantine province, and from there across North Africa and into Spain. As they advanced they brought with them the Islamic religion and the Arabic language. The majority of the peoples they conquered accepted both in time but it was the religion which was the more extensive. The language and culture of the Persians survived their conquest by the Arabs and their acceptance of the Islamic faith, although the Farsi language adopted the Arabic script and an extensive Arabic vocabulary.

Within thirty years of the prophet's death, decisive events were to shape the future of Islam and of the prophet's Arabian homeland. In AD 656 the caliph Omar's successor, Othman, was assassinated and his natural successor seemed to be Ali, first cousin of the prophet and husband of his daughter Fatima. But Ali was opposed by the ambitious and able Arab general Muawiya, whom Omar had appointed governor of Syria and, like Othman, belonged to the powerful Umayyad family of Mecca. The defeat of Ali and his son Hussein by the Umayyads led to the first and only great division in Islam: between the Sunnis, or 'people of the Sunnah', who are the great majority, and the Shia, or 'partisans' of Ali, who continue to regard Muawiya and his Umayyad successors as secular usurpers.

In the Arabian Peninsula the great majority of the people have remained Sunni, although there are important Shiite minorities on the eastern fringes, and the Zaydis, who inhabit the Yemeni mountains, belong to a branch of Shiism. But Sunnism and Shiism continued in dispute in Persia until, in the sixteenth century, Shiism was adopted as its ruling faith. This has a significant bearing on the modern history of the Gulf region.

The triumph of the Umayyads not only caused the split in Islam; it made Damascus the capital of the new Arab/Islamic empire. After a century, the defeat of the Ummayyads by the Abbasids moved the centre of power to Baghdad, inaugurating the 'Golden Age of Islam'. The Hejaz region of western Arabia retained its importance as the source of Islam and the object of its veneration. To the east, the Gulf remained a principal route for Arab traders to India and China. But it was the great Muslim cities to the north and west of Arabia – Aleppo, Damascus, Baghdad and Cairo – which were the centres of Islamic material wealth and power. When the Christian West made its first combined onslaught on the world of Islam with the Crusades, the prolonged battle was fought out in the lands of the eastern Mediter-ranean, and it was there that victory was ultimately won – a victory at a terrible cost, from which the world of Islam never fully recovered.

In the first great Arab/Islamic expansion the fighting was done only by the Beduin Arab warriors. At this stage those of pure Arab descent formed the ruling caste among Muslims; the Islamic state was essentially an Arab confederation. Non-Arabs who accepted Islam, such as Persians, Egyptians or North African Berbers, or even Arabs who had failed to prove their membership of the dominant caste, were known as *mawalis*, or clients. However, with the need for increased manpower as the empire grew, this was bound to change. The *mawalis* began to swell the ranks of the Muslim armies and, as Muslim society became increasingly multi-racial, the distinction disappeared. Saladin, the great victor of the Crusades, was a Kurd. In fact, the very meaning of the word 'Arab' gradually changed; today it is normally applied to all the peoples of the Arabic-speaking countries, many of whom have very little 'pure' Arab blood in their veins.

As the Abbasid empire declined a further trend began which led to the domination of the Islamic world by men for whom Arabic was not even their first language. From about the middle of the ninth century AD, the caliph's army, which now consisted of paid troops instead of mounted tribesmen spurred by faith in Islam and the lure of booty, was increasingly recruited from among the Turks. Some of these were free men but others were Turkish and Circassian slaves from central Asia who were specially trained for the purpose; they became known as Mamlukes (Arabic *mamluk*, or 'owned'). They were taught to be Muslims and trained in total devotion to the caliph, but as they became more indispensable their desire for power increased. Gradually they encroached upon the government until they became a ruling caste with king-making powers.

In the middle of the eleventh century AD, a tribal confederation of central Asian nomads who had recently been converted to Islam – the Seljuks – conquered Syria and the greater part of Anatolia (which had always eluded the grasp of the Arabs). The period in which they were able to maintain a reunited Islamic empire was brief but they inaugurated an era of some eight hundred years in which the Turks were to be the dominant element in Islam. By the end of the thirteenth century, Othman, a Turkish mercenary recently converted to Islam, had laid the foundations in Asia Minor of a new Islamic empire which steadily expanded its dominion over most of the Arabic-speaking world. By the early sixteenth century all the Arab heartlands – Mecca, Medina, Syria and Egypt – had come under Ottoman Turkish control. Although the Ottomans captured Baghdad in 1534 and Basra in 1546, Mesopotamia (or Iraq) continued to be the subject of dispute with the Shiite dynasty of the Safavids in Persia for another two centuries until it was finally incorporated into the Ottoman empire.

After the Ottoman Turks had captured Constantinople in 1453 and overthrown the Byzantine empire, the main struggle of this new Islamic power was with Christian Europe, which it more than matched in strength. For some time the Turks showed relatively little interest in the Arabian Peninsula. They allowed the Arab *sharifs* (or princes) of Mecca to maintain their autonomy, which enabled them to build up considerable power and prestige for themselves among the desert tribes. The Turks spent considerable sums on the improvement of the caravan routes and the repair and adornment of the Holy Places, but it was only some two centuries later that the Ottoman sultans assumed the title of caliphs of Islam.

The Turks gained control of Yemen but were expelled by the mountain tribesmen during the early seventeenth century. In eastern Arabia their hold was even lighter.

Muslim historians and geographers are the main source of information about the Gulf during the nine centuries since it had become part of the Islamic world. From them we know that it flourished as a trade route and that, at least from the tenth century AD, Arab ships from the Gulf were sailing as far as Madagascar and China, while Chinese junks were appearing in Gulf waters. From an early stage, attempts were made to assist navigation. The Persian writer Nasir-i-Khusraw recorded in the eleventh century that *khashabat*, or wooden posts, were placed at the northern end of the Gulf:

They are erected for a double purpose: firstly, for lighting during the night; by means of lights enclosed in glass to protect them from the wind, to warn vessels to take precautions in these dangerous waters; and secondly, to show the navigator his position, and to warn him against possible pirates.

From classical times there were always towns of importance in this region at the head of the Gulf where the Tigris and the Euphrates meet the sea and the trade routes from Najd, Syria and Persia converge. After his defeat of the Persians, the caliph Omar gave orders for the foundation of Basra (that is, old Basra, which was some miles from the present city) to command the approaches to Iraq from the sea. Under the Abbasids, Basra was the most important port in the Gulf, although it gradually fell into decline along with their empire.

Southwards along the Arab coast of the Gulf there was only a small settled population. The most important centre was Hajar, which included the islands of Bahrain and the oasis district of al-Hasa near the coast (which is now part of Saudi Arabia). Here they cultivated corn, cotton, dates and other fruit, and fished pearls. The Arab traveller Ibn Battuta reported that the dates were so abundant that at al-Hasa they were used to feed the cattle.

The Ottoman Turks arrived and occupied al-Hasa in 1536. But they had been preceded in the Gulf by a very different kind of power – the Portuguese. In 1498 the great Portuguese mariner Vasco da Gama had reached India via the Cape of Good Hope and returned to Lisbon laden with spices. In reducing the importance of the overland trade routes from Europe to the East, this new route helped to turn the great commercial centres of the Muslim world into economic backwaters. Its establishment was ultimately one of the major reasons for the economic domination of the Muslim world by the West.

With their ambitions to build a great empire in India and the East, the Portuguese aimed to dominate the Red Sea and the Arabian Gulf. Fired by a combination of anti-Islamic fervour and commercial greed, they had arrived in the Gulf some thirty years before the Turks. They attacked and pillaged the Arabian coast from Muscat to Bahrain, leaving forts and garrisons to dominate the indigenous Arab trading and pearling communities. Throughout the sixteenth century the Portuguese controlled trade through the Gulf and the Straits of Hormuz. From time to time the

Turks, with the help of local tribes, were able to challenge their supremacy. They drove the Turks out of Bahrain and Muscat. But eventually it was the superiority of the Portuguese fleet that counted. The real challenge to the Portuguese came from two rival European maritime powers, England and Holland. By the end of the sixteenth century Dutch and English adventurers (or pirates) were beginning to compete for the spice trade. Early in the seventeenth century both the English East India Company and the Dutch East India Company were formed and, with licences from the shah of Persia, began to trade on a regular basis. Throughout the seventeenth century it was the Dutch who were dominant, but by 1750 the British had become supreme. In 1698 the English had agreed with the Dutch and the French to share responsibility for policing the Gulf waters, but the whole responsibility passed to the English when in the eighteenth century India became largely a British possession and the French and Dutch were ousted from the subcontinent.

3

The Rise of Kuwait

In the crucial years when the Kuwaitis, under the leadership of the al-Sabah family, were establishing themselves as an independent entity, they were helped by the lack of any stable centralizing power in the region. The Persian empire was in confusion, while the Mameluke rulers of Iraq were largely independent of the Ottoman sultan in Constantinople. Although Kuwait was nominally part of the Ottoman empire, the Kuwaitis easily persuaded the local Turkish administrator in Basra to leave them in peace. Eastern Arabia was under the control of the Bani Khalid, but they did nothing to prevent Kuwait's independent development, while their protection of the caravan routes benefited trade. The British at this stage, and for some time to come, were interested only in their maritime commercial interests in the region.

Like all the nomadic tribesmen who settled on the coast, the Utub found that they had not only to learn a new way of life in trading, seafaring, fishing and pearling, but also to adapt their political organization. They divided themselves into three roughly equal groups, one to administer the affairs of the community, another to trade, and a third to fish for pearls, with all three of them sharing the profits. This established a principle of power-sharing which has survived to the present day.

Kuwait began to prosper under its new ruler, Shaikh Sabah (c. 1752–64). A mud wall was built around the town for protection, and authority was extended into the interior and over Failaka and other offshore islands. Early visitors noted evidence of the Kuwaitis' success as traders and pearlers. Carstin Niebuhr of the 1760 Danish expedition reported that Kuwait had a fleet of eight hundred small ships.

When Shaikh Sabah died in 1764, his youngest son, Abdallah, was elected by the other Utub families to succeed him. This established another lasting precedent that the most suitable member of the Sabah family should be chosen as the new ruler. Primogeniture has never been an Arab tradition.

When Shaikh Abdallah died after a reign of some fifty years, the Utub, who were now dominant in both Kuwait and Bahrain, had become the principal Arab navigators in the Gulf. Kuwait received an additional boost from the Persian occupation of Basra between 1775 and 1779, which caused the diversion of trade between India and the West from Basra to Kuwait.

At the end of the eighteenth century, however, Kuwait had to face a new threat to its independent existence which was to last intermittently until modern times.

This arose from Najd. The tribesmen of central Arabia had never been fully converted to the Islamic faith and by the 1700s had either adopted various heresies or reverted to pre-Islamic idolatry. Wadi Hanifah in central Najd saw the birth of a great religious reformer, Muhammad ibn Abd al-Wahhab, who dedicated himself to preaching the essential Islamic doctrine of unitarianism or *tawhid* – that is, the oneness of God and the elimination of all traces of polytheism. In 1744 he formed an alliance with Muhammad ibn Saud, Amir of Diraiyah, an oasis in Wadi Hanifah, and this laid the first foundation of the present kingdom of Saudi Arabia.

The union between militant reformism and a powerful desert warrior created a potent new force in Arabia. By the 1790s the Wahhabis (or *Muwahhidoun*, i.e. unitarians, as they prefer to be known) had occupied al-Hasa. Through a judicious mixture of firmness and diplomacy the young Kuwaiti state survived, although it probably had to recognize a form of Wahhabi suzerainty.

During the nineteenth century, as Wahhabi power rose and fell more than once, Kuwait was frequently under pressure which it had to learn every available means to resist.

Under Shaikh Abdallah the separation of powers in the Kuwaiti community had reached a new stage of development as the Sabah family gave up sharing in the merchants' profits in order to devote themselves entirely to the affairs of government. In return they levied a duty of about one per cent on all imports. This delegation of governmental authority to the Sabah was carried out, as always, with the agreement of the other Utub families. Shaikh Abdallah's son Jaber, who succeeded, also had a long reign (1815–58), and during this time Kuwait continued to increase in prosperity. Its population rose to 25,000 and its fleet of larger vessels traded regularly into the Indian Ocean and the Red Sea. Imports consisted of piece goods, rice, sugar, timber, spices and cotton from India; coffee from the Red Sea; tobacco and dried fruits from Persia; grain and dates from Basra; cloth, dates and fish from Bahrain. The exports were ghee and horses from the inland tribes for India, and local dried and salt fish for Basra. According to an 1845 report, Shaikh Jaber's income from the one per cent duty on imports was about 3000 dollars annually.

The members of the al-Sabah chose who should be the head of the family and therefore the Amir of Kuwait. But he was far from being an absolute ruler. On his election the ruler always gave his *ahd*, or pledge, to rule justly and in accordance with the Islamic principle of *shura*, or consultation, and on this condition the leading merchants would come to him on the following day to pledge their allegiance. The Kuwaiti historian Al-Rashid described the system:

The ruler consulted the notables on the important issues at hand particularly on how to safeguard the country against unexpected outside attacks, and had no choice but to accept their decisions since real authority rested with them and not with the ruler whom they only allowed to be their chief out of courtesy.

The emir was less wealthy than a number of the leading merchants, who also formed the most highly educated element in Kuwaiti society. The merchants were relatively few in number and included both the wealthy pearl merchants and importers and the small retailers. The great majority of Kuwaitis worked at sea either as merchant sailors, pearlers or fishermen. In spite of the importance of the marine trade, the pearling industry was the basis of the wealth of the most prominent merchants.

The pearlers led hard lives during the four-month summer season when they were away from home. Instead of wages they received an advance on future profits from the ships' captains who in turn borrowed from the pearl merchants, usually at exorbitant rates of interest. Most of the divers were in debt and many were elderly men who had to go on diving to survive.

The other element in Kuwait society was formed by the beduin, who in many ways regarded themselves as distinct. They carried arms and enjoyed a special relationship with the ruling family, for whose security they were responsible; today they still play a dominant role in the police force.

Some of Kuwait's amirs have naturally been more masterful and dominating than others. But they have never been despots. They have acted rather as arbiters in the settlement of disputes between the different elements in Kuwaiti society. Such settlements always achieved the minimum of consensus needed for a stable and enduring political community.

Throughout the nineteenth century Kuwait was generally well served by its rulers, who handled external dangers with skill and determination. There were various alarms and threats, such as when the Turco-Egyptians who had overthrown the Saudi/Wahhabi state in central Arabia endeavoured to establish their hegemony in eastern Arabia in 1839–40. The Egyptians did not stay long but their departure meant a partial revival of Saudi power. However, the House of Saud was divided; Kuwait remained determinedly neutral, granting asylum to the members of the family who had been defeated and sought refuge.

In 1871 the Ottoman Turks returned with more lasting determination. This time the Kuwaiti amir, Shaikh Abdallah, sent troops in to join the Turkish expedition to occupy al-Hasa and was rewarded with the Ottoman appointment of *qaimmaqam*, or provincial governor. This did not mean that Kuwait's independence was lost; the title was more decorative than administrative. The truth was that it served the Turkish interest that Kuwait should remain outside the control of the other major power in the Gulf – Britain.

Since the beginning of the nineteenth century a Pax Britannica had been gradually enforced and extended in the Gulf, which was one of the principal routes between Europe and India. It was above all Britain's possessions and interests in India which made Britain a world power and even after the opening of the Suez Canal in 1869 the Gulf retained much of its importance to Britain as a route for trade and mail.

Britain's first concern was to keep down piracy, and with this object it succeeded in 1820 in concluding a General Treaty of Maritime Peace in perpetuity with the small states of the Trucial Coast (the United Arab Emirates of today) and Bahrain. Britain did not attempt to include Kuwait in the treaty because the Kuwaitis were not engaged in piracy. Other agreements followed but at this stage Britain still had no interest in interfering in the internal affairs of the Arab Gulf states. It was Ottoman Turkey's re-entry on the scene which made Britain realize that it could not set its own limits to its involvement. If the Turks had employed only land forces to assert their control over eastern Arabia, the British would have disliked it but accepted that there was nothing they could do about it. It was the use of Turkish naval power in the waters of what Britain was coming to regard as a British lake that caused the real concern. As the foreign secretary in the British government of India pointed out to the viceroy in May 1871, 'If the Arab chiefs, remaining quiet now, wish hereafter to fit out some naval force, how are we to prevent them when we have permitted the Turks to do so, or how are we to make the prohibition intelligible? Or, if Persia, desirous to have a fleet in the Gulf to establish her claims to supremacy, should throw herself on some foreign power and procure vessels of war, on what grounds are we to remonstrate?'

Accordingly, Britain went on to sign a series of so-called exclusive agreements with the rulers of the Arab Gulf states. The agreement signed with the ruler of Bahrain in 1880 provided the model. It bound the ruler and his successors

to abstain from entering into negotiations or making treaties of any sort with any State or Government other than the British without the consent of the said British Government, and to refuse permission to any other Government than the British to establish diplomatic or consular agencies or coal depots in [his] territory, unless with the consent of the British Government.

Kuwait was still not included in these agreements because Britain saw no threat to its interests if Kuwait remained under a very loose form of Turkish suzerainty. In this case the situation was to change because of the advent of a ruler of Kuwait who saw an agreement with Britain as the best way of preserving and reinforcing his country's independence. This was Mubarak the Great (1896–1915), generally regarded as the founder of modern Kuwait.

Mubarak's reign had a troubled beginning. A fierce family feud resulted in the death of two of Mubarak's brothers who had combined against him. The event was a cause of great sadness in Kuwait because, although such violence was common enough among the ruling families of eastern Arabia, it had not occurred with the Sabah (and would not do so again). Recognizing the inevitable, the merchants gave Mubarak their allegiance.

As expected, Mubarak set about vigorously and even aggressively defending Kuwait's interests. His force of 25,000 tribesmen made sure that no attack on a Kuwaiti caravan or any of the beduin tribes under his protection went unpunished. But this was not enough to ensure Kuwait's safety from the ambitions of the Ottomans to assert their control, and shortly after his succession Mubarak sought an agreement with the British. At first Britain refused, on the grounds that the *status quo* was satisfactory, but two years later it changed its mind. In December 1898 the Ottoman government had granted a Russian Count Kapnist a concession to build a railway from the Syrian coast via Baghdad to Kuwait; this posed a clear Russian threat to the route to India. At about the same time Lord Curzon, an expert on the region and a vigorous British imperialist, with powerful support in London, was appointed viceroy of India. In 1899 Britain signed an agreement with Shaikh Mubarak which included an undertaking that the shaikh, his heirs and successors would not 'cede, sell, lease, mortgage or give for occupation or any other purpose any portion of his territory to the Government or subjects of any other power' without the previous consent of the British government. There was no clause in the agreement guaranteeing Britain's defence of Kuwait, although this was clearly understood by all those concerned. The agreement came just in time for Britain to forestall a German plan, rivalling that of the Russians, to extend the new Berlin–Istanbul railway through Baghdad to the Gulf at Kuwait.

This agreement gave Mubarak the security he needed for the consolidation of Kuwait. But there were limits to what more he could achieve in eastern Arabia. The head of the House of Saud, Abdul Rahman ibn Faisal, had taken refuge in Kuwait after his defeat by his rivals, the Rashidis. Mubarak helped him in his efforts to restore the Saudi state but with indifferent success. It was the youthful son of Abdul Rahman – Abdul Aziz ('Ibn Saud') – who left Kuwait to recapture the Saudi capital, Riyadh, and went on not only to restore the Saudi position in Najd but to drive the Turks out of al-Hasa before the outbreak of the First World War. Mubarak remained on good terms with Abdul Aziz but any plans he had entertained for Kuwait's expansion into eastern Arabia were frustrated by this outstanding young desert leader.

At home Kuwait grew and prospered under Mubarak. The population doubled during his reign with the help of immigration from Arabia, Iraq and Iran. In 1913 Kuwait's pearling industry, with its fleet of more than eight hundred, reached its peak in what became known as *sanat at-tahfa* (the year of superabundance). Postal and telegraph services were established, and in 1901 the British India Steam Navigation Company set up an agency at Kuwait which became a port of call for their steamers. In 1911 the al-Mubarakiya School was founded to teach a modern as well as traditional syllabus, and in the same year an Arabian American mission, after British suspicions of this transatlantic intrusion had been overcome, laid the foundations of a medical service.

There were internal problems when Mubarak's vigorous foreign policy created a need for higher revenues. As he sharply increased taxation the leading merchants resisted. Eventually a compromise was reached whereby control of the economy remained in the merchants' hands, although for the time being their vital role in providing political advice to the ruler was abandoned. After his rule the situation reverted to what it had been before.

Through the 1899 agreement Mubarak had delegated his foreign policy to Britain, and when in 1913 Britain negotiated an agreement with the Ottomans defining the borders between Kuwait, Najd and Iraq he accepted them. When the Turks allied themselves with Germany in the First World War, he declared for Britain and helped to persuade Abdul Aziz, now Sultan of Najd and its dependencies, to do likewise. Salim, the second of his two sons who succeeded him, had some sympathies with the Turks as fellow Muslims but he was unable to declare them openly. Throughout the war

Kuwait benefited greatly as the main port of entry to Syria, which was blockaded by the allies from the Mediterranean.

It was under Salem (1917–21) that Kuwait faced the most severe test of its existence. Sultan Abdul Aziz (Ibn Saud) did not accept the borders between Najd and Kuwait that had been laid down by the agreement between Britain and the Ottomans. Shaikh Salem's refusal to allow Ibn Saud's agent to collect customs and transit dues from Najdi merchants in Kuwait who were exporting to Najd caused Ibn Saud to place an embargo on trade with Kuwait which was to last for twenty years and cause Kuwait great damage. Also, Ibn Saud's puritanical Wahhabi warriors – the Ikhwan – regarded the Kuwaitis as intolerably loose-living. Sporadic raids by the Ikhwan culminated in a full-scale attack under their leader, Faisal al-Darwish, in October 1920. Salem rallied his troops and went out to meet them at Jahra, some thirty miles east of Kuwait City. The Kuwaitis suffered severe loss of life but their resistance halted the Saudi advance until the arrival of British warships and the landing of marines caused the Ikhwan to withdraw. Shaikh Salim died the following year and was succeeded by his nephew Ahmad, who was to prove another able ruler.

With the defeat of Turkey and Germany in 1918, Britain was left in an unchallenged position in the Gulf. Britain and France had already made plans to partition the former Arab provinces of the Ottoman empire between them but France's concerns in the Arab world were concentrated on the Maghreb and the Levant states. Their United States ally, after playing a leading role in the Paris Peace Conference following the war, withdrew into isolation. The Russians had already abandoned their imperial interests in the Middle East after the 1917 Bolshevik revolution.

In Iraq, for which a British mandate had been secured from the League of Nations, Britain installed a monarchy of the Hashemites, the Arab rulers of Mecca who launched the revolt against the Turks with British encouragement. Britain by now had exclusive agreements with all the Arab Gulf shaikhdoms. In the Arabian Peninsula it was providing subsidies to the two main powers – Hussein, the Hashemite king of Hejaz, and Ibn Saud, sultan of Najd. But there were still difficult frontier problems to be resolved. The 1913 agreement with the Ottoman Turks was no longer applicable and in any case had never been ratified.

The British high commissioner in Iraq, Sir Percy Cox, arranged a meeting with Ibn Saud at Uqair, the seaport of al-Hasa. The British resident in Kuwait attended to represent Kuwait's interests. Cox drew the frontiers which gave Iraq a large slice of territory claimed by Iraq and, in order to placate Ibn Saud, he allocated to Najd some two-thirds of the land that had been considered to belong to Kuwait at the time of the 1913 agreement. An embarrassed Cox later explained to Shaikh Ahmad that nothing could be done to prevent Ibn Saud from taking this territory if he wished, but he added that if Kuwait was able to win it back Britain would do nothing to stand in the way.

In his different way, Shaikh Ahmad, who ruled from 1921 to 1950, was as remarkable as Mubarak. He was less ambitious and took fewer risks. He was aware that Kuwait needed the help of more powerful friends and neighbours to preserve its independence but he was both stubborn and subtle in his diplomatic use of the assets that Kuwait possessed. One of these was the secure knowledge that the other powers in the region preferred that Kuwait should be independent rather than swallowed up by the rest.

Ahmad had a striking presence. Amin Rihani describes him in his English book *Around the Coasts of Arabia* as:

of medium height and prepossessing. He is meticulous in dress, soft of voice, elegant in gesture, and more Aryan than Semitic in type. Were it not for his sandals and his Arab clothes he might be taken for a Muslim from the Punjab or European from Spain.

In the chapter on Shaikh Ahmad in his Arabic book *Muluk al-Arab* (*Kings of the Arabs*) Rihani pointed out that his gentle manner and preference for conciliation did not belie his courage and determination in moment of crisis. Rihani also emphasized what he saw as the most important feature of Kuwait. He said that, despite Kuwait's preoccupations with commerce and politics, the state had another form of wealth apart from pearls: the intelligence and culture of which he had seen so many fine examples at Shaikh Ahmad's *majlis* (Council) and receptions. He said that the cultural renaissance had two main foundations – the national library and the day and night schools – and that it drew benefit from modern developments in the arts and sciences in Syria and Egypt. It reached parts of the country which were without newspapers, magazines or books because there were still no schools. Rihani concluded that, just as Kuwaiti sailing ships reached ports which large steamers could not enter, so educated Kuwaitis were spreading the spirit of science and learning during their travels among the beduin and the more remote settled areas of Arabia.

A superficial view of the history of the Arab Gulf in the two centuries before the modern era gives the impression that it was cut off from the rest of the Arab world. This is because, except for brief periods, the political relations between the states were minimal. But in fact the peoples of the region never ceased to interact with their neighbours – through the constant moves of population and the exchanges of cultural and religious life. Kuwait played a crucial role in this exchange.

During Shaikh Ahmad's reign Kuwait's future as the first of the oil city-states was decided. The thirteen years of negotiations which ended with the granting of the Kuwait Oil Company's concession demonstrate Ahmad's supreme diplomatic skill and his ability to make the best of a weak hand.

The British had first shown interest in Kuwait's possibilities as a source of oil during the reign of Shaikh Mubarak before the First World War. Seepages of bitumen were clearly visible at Burgan and Bahra. In 1911 Mr Greenway, managing director of the Anglo-Persian Oil Company (APOC), wrote to the British political resident in Bushire to ask his opinion as to whether 'a valid concession for working oil in Kuwait' was obtainable from Mubarak. But the British government considered that disturbed relations between Turks and Arabs in this corner of the Ottoman empire would make an oil exploration concession unworkable. A British Admiralty commission visited Kuwait in 1913 and an APOC geologist in the following year. Both recommended (quite justifiably, it was to turn out later) that drilling should concentrate on the Burgan plain. But the political resident's advice was taken that nothing could be done until after the war was over.

The great powers had become aware of the importance of oil before the war. The United States had a virtual monopoly of supplies until the first important Middle East discovery at Masjid al-Sulaiman in south-western Persia in 1908. The following year APOC took over the concession and commercial production began in 1912. By this time the young Winston Churchill had become first lord of the admiralty in Britain's Liberal government; he was determined to help the first sea lord, Admiral John Fisher, to realize the long-held dream of converting the entire Royal Navy from the use of coal to oil which caused Fisher to be known as the 'oil maniac'. A vast three-year programme achieved this by the outbreak of war. When the war was over Lord Curzon made his celebrated remark that the allies had 'floated to victory on a sea of oil'.

Winston Churchill had been acutely conscious that there was no major source of oil anywhere in the British empire. Accordingly, he managed to push through the British parliament an agreement whereby Britain acquired a controlling interest in APOC (later the Anglo-Iranian Oil Company and ultimately British Petroleum). The original investment of £2.2 million, in Churchill's own words, 'brought us a prize from fairyland far beyond our brightest hopes'. It paid for the entire naval programme. It also for a time made southern Persia part of Britain's quasi-empire in the Middle East.

The war showed that oil was not only important but vital for survival. 'Oil is as necessary as blood', said Clemenceau, the French premier.

The advent of peace brought a new surge in the demand for oil with the spread of the motorcar and the growth of oil-based industries. In the West a new era had begun which was based on the consumption of cheap oil. The United States was far the largest producer as well as consumer but, despite the boundless optimism of the Americans in the 1920s, they were aware that their resources were not limitless. As the experts warned that reserves were being rapidly depleted, the oil companies began to look for new sources from abroad. Increasingly they were able to secure the diplomatic support of the US government.

However, the United States's former allies – Britain and France – had already partitioned between them the most promising oil-bearing region outside the United States: the Middle East. Of the two, Britain, with its dominance in Persia, Iraq and the Gulf, was in the stronger position. The two European powers had every intention of excluding the United States, which they felt already had enough oil of its own in Texas. Understandably, the United States did not agree. Instead it declared the doctrine of the 'open door', which meant that the wartime allies should not discriminate against each other in oil supplies. As Anthony Sampson commented in his classic anatomy of the world system created by the major oil companies, *The Seven Sisters*:

It was a plausible liberal policy, but over the following years the Open Door proved to be a mysterious portal, with a habit of swinging shut again, just as the Americans had got inside.

Britain was in a good position to defend Kuwait against an American invasion because of its exclusive agreement. In 1913 Shaikh Mubarak had accepted in a letter to the British political resident that no Kuwait oil concession would be given except to a person nominated and recommended by the British government. Before the war ended APOC wrote to the British Foreign Office applying for an oil concession covering 'such parts of Mesopotamia' as might come under British control after the war. At the same time it asked for such a concession to be extended to Kuwait. The Foreign Office (and later the Colonial Office, which took over responsibility for Kuwaiti affairs after the war) agreed but insisted that all negotiations for a concession with the ruler of Kuwait should be conducted through the British political resident, who was instructed accordingly. However, for two reasons APOC showed only a limp interest in Kuwait at that time. One was simply that the company already had all the oil it needed on its hands in

Persia. The other was that the company's geologists were convinced that, despite the seepages of bitumen in Kuwait, only the eastern side of the Gulf would yield oil in commercial quantities. The western shores of the Gulf lacked the Oligocene–Miocene formation found in Persia and Iraq. However, this did not mean that either the British government or APOC were happy to see a concession granted to a non-British company. They were two dogs in the Kuwaiti manger.

By early 1923 some leisurely negotiations with Shaikh Ahmad were being conducted by APOC through the British political agent in Kuwait. Ahmad's reaction was that the company's offers for exploration licences were reasonable but that the fixed royalty proposed for subsequent production was much too small. He wanted a '25% royalty on net crude oil'.

Suddenly a vigorous challenge to APOC's complacency arrived from an unexpected quarter. Major Frank Holmes, a colourful New Zealand adventurer and promoter, who had served in the British navy in the war and mined in most parts of the world, had just won an exploration concession for the al-Hasa region from Sultan Ibn Saud for his own little company, Eastern and General Syndicates. (Amin Rihani, who was present at the negotiations, had strongly urged his case with the Saudi leader.) APOC was convinced that there was even less likelihood of oil in al-Hasa than in Bahrain or Kuwait and did not take the threat seriously. However, Holmes, who had learned about Kuwait from a Kuwaiti member of Ibn Saud's entourage, now sent a cable to Shaikh Ahmad urging him not to grant any oil concessions until he had seen the terms offered by his company. Holmes was indeed offering better terms than APOC and he arrived in Kuwait to present them personally to Shaikh Ahmad and lay the foundations of a friendship which was to last a lifetime. Holmes knew no Arabic and was a stranger to the region. He cut a bizarre figure when he arrived to negotiate with Ibn Saud carrying an enormous green-lined white umbrella and wearing a French-style pith helmet. But many Arabs found his humorous, unstuffy personality attractive, and Shaikh Ahmad was no exception.

Delighted that he was no longer dealing with a monopoly, Shaikh Ahmad showed his customary skill in negotiation. When the British political agent reminded him of his obligation not to negotiate oil concessions except with persons nominated and approved by the British government, he replied that Holmes was a British subject who had offered better terms than APOC and was on his way to London to present them to the British government.

In this way negotiations were prolonged for more than a decade. The

British Colonial Office still wanted to give APOC priority but warned the company that it could not do so indefinitely. In May 1924 Shaikh Ahmad strengthened his hand by signing jointly with Ibn Saud a concession agreement with Holmes's EGS covering the Saudi Arabia/Kuwait neutral zone. On a visit to APOC's installations in southern Persia, Shaikh Ahmad blandly explained that he had had no alternative because of his political relations with the Saudi leader. A year later Holmes also secured a new concession from the ruler of Bahrain.

However, Holmes still lacked the essential backing of finance and expertise to exploit his oil concessions. With the geologists' reports still discouraging, in a moment of uncustomary pessimism Holmes offered to sell to APOC all his concessionary rights in al-Hasa, Bahrain, the neutral zone and any he might hope to receive for Kuwait, for £50,000 to compensate him for all his expenses in obtaining them. APOC made a lower counter-offer, which Holmes refused, and then broke off the negotiations. The company was not really interested.

In 1927 the situation was again transformed as the indefatigable Holmes was able to secure the backing of the giant Gulf Oil Corporation of Pennsylvania, which bought options to acquire all Holmes's concessions. In Kuwait Holmes had been drilling for water under a contract which he had negotiated with Shaikh Ahmad in 1926. In one of the wells there were traces of oil. He kept this secret but informed Gulf Oil, which until then had been reluctant to consider entering such an uncertain region. Holmes was now able to inform Shaikh Ahmad that he had the support of major American interests. Ahmad was favourably impressed but Holmes was surprised when he offered what he considered to be highly favourable terms for a concession on Gulf's behalf and Shaikh Ahmad refused. He should not have been surprised. With the backing of his council and Kuwaiti public opinion, Shaikh Ahmad was determined to keep the bargaining going. He was also aware that Britain would use its special relationship with Kuwait to try to keep out the Americans. The most subtle diplomacy was still required.

Britain did as expected. In November 1928 the political agent informed Holmes that the British government would require the insertion in any oil concession which Shaikh Ahmad might grant of a 'British nationality clause' which effectively excluded all non-British companies.

The bargaining remained stalled for three years. This was the time of the great depression and all the major oil companies were cutting back on their expenditure. It was also a time of depression in Kuwait. Several pearling seasons had failed and the general decline in commerce was aggravated by the Saudi blockade of Kuwaiti trade with the interior of Arabia. By now Shaikh Ahmad was anxious to close a deal to alleviate the country's distress.

Fortunately Kuwait's bargaining position began to improve. US oil companies, backed by the US government, succeeded in persuading the British government to revise the 'nationality clause' it was also trying to impose in Bahrain and to allow American companies to participate in a Bahraini concession. An agreement was signed by the ruler of Bahrain with the Bahrain Petroleum Company (Bapco), a subsidiary of Standard Oil of California. The fiction of British nationality was maintained by having Bapco incorporated in Canada. However, a precedent had been set for allowing American participation in Kuwait and at this point US pressure in Britain was intensified by the appointment early in 1932 as ambassador in London of Andrew Mellon, who had helped found Bapco and whose family still owned a large number of the company's shares. In April 1932 the British government conceded the US request for an 'open door' policy for US oil companies in Kuwait.

In June 1932, the situation was suddenly transformed by the discovery of oil in commercial quantities in Bahrain. Holmes's conviction that, despite the opinion of the oil company geologists, there were large oil deposits on the Arabian side of the Gulf had been proved right. To Shaikh Ahmad's delight, the competition between Gulf Oil and APOC for a Kuwaiti concession now became intense. But negotiations lasted another two years as Shaikh Ahmad sought to secure the best possible terms. The pace quickened in 1933 as Ibn Saud, now king of Saudi Arabia, granted an oil concession to Standard Oil of California. The Saudi monarch had always felt a preference for American oil companies over the European companies, which he associated with the old-style colonialism in the Arab and Islamic countries. Although his position differed from that of Shaikh Ahmad in that he was free from any treaty obligation to Britain, his choice undoubtedly strengthened Ahmad's bargaining power. APOC and Gulf Oil then announced their latest move. After lengthy negotiations behind the scenes they had decided to end their hostilities and form an alliance to negotiate jointly as equal partners for a concession. For this purpose they formed the jointly owned Kuwait Oil Company (KOC).

Faced with this powerful alliance which might have been expected to be able to dictate its own terms, Shaikh Ahmad was provided with a new weapon in the form of a rival bid from a third company. This was Traders Ltd, a company put together by a group of right-wing, imperial-minded British politicians and businessmen led by Lord Lloyd (former high commissioner in Egypt) with the specific aim of keeping the Gulf '100 per cent British' by excluding the American oil companies. The company announced its formation on 5 April 1932, the day before the British government decided in favour of the 'open door' policy in Kuwait.

It is probable that Shaikh Ahmad knew that he would ultimately grant the concession to KOC. It was his wish that an American oil company should be involved and he could certainly see the danger of granting a monopoly to a company such as Traders Ltd which was dedicated to maintaining the Gulf as a British preserve. But Shaikh Ahmad was quite prepared to use the Traders' bid to extract the best possible terms from KOC, even in matters of detail relating to the method of payment of royalties, his right to appoint a KOC director and the level of such a director's salary. He was helped by the fact that both Gulf and APOC regarded Traders as a serious competitor and were aware that it could press its case in the British parliament, where it might accuse the British government of weakening Britain's position in the Gulf. In his account *The First Kuwait Oil Concession* (London, 1975) A.H.T. Chisholm, the chief negotiator for APOC, provides an extraordinary picture of Shaikh Ahmad's untiring application to the business of negotiating an agreement on which so much of the country's future depended. With the help of his able Iraqi lawyer, J. Gabriel, he attained a high level of expertise in the details of the oil business. Chisholm describes at one point how Shaikh Ahmad, as was his custom, requested him and Holmes to give 'their fullest reasons and arguments' for the three major points being put forward by the Kuwait Oil Company. When they had done so the Shaikh paused for reflection for so long that they knew from their previous experience that 'a very unfavourable reply was about to be given'; indeed, he answered 'with even more than his usual air of dignified determination'.

On one point Shaikh Ahmad was not prepared to compromise. In March 1934, shortly after KOC had been incorporated, the new company had made a separate political agreement with the British government. This contained clauses providing that KOC should remain a British company (despite the 50 % US ownership) and that the concession could never be transferred without the consent of the British government. It also gave Britain the right of pre-emption over Kuwait oil and oil products in the event of war and a large measure of control over the nationality of the company's employees, and landing rights and wireless facilities for company aircraft. Finally the agreement laid down the general principle that, should there be any conflict between the terms of the agreement and concession granted to KOC by the shaikh, the former should take precedence.

The KOC negotiators and the British government wanted this last point to be included formally in the concession agreement. Shaikh Ahmad was adamant, saying with good reason that this meant that any of the terms in his concession could be overruled by a political agreement to which he was not a party and which had been made without his knowledge. Moreover the matter would become public property as soon as the terms of the concession were published. It was therefore beneath his dignity even to consider the inclusion of such a clause.

The negotiators advised London of Shaikh Ahmad's objections and eventually the British government gave way. Britain's special position in Kuwait, and hence its continuing ability to exercise some control over the relationship between Kuwait and any oil company operating in its territory, remained a reality; this was referred to in a separate correspondence between Shaikh Ahmad and the British government. But Shaikh Ahmad had gained a point of vital importance. Kuwait's relations with Britain would change in time. The form of the relationship between Kuwait and Britain which had been established in 1899 would not be enshrined in a concession made in 1934.

Eventually the way was clear for the signing of the agreement, which took place in Kuwait on 23 December 1934. It covered the whole of Kuwait's approximately 6000 square miles of territory and was to last for seventy-five years.

The amounts of money involved seem derisory today. In return for exemption from all taxes, the concessionaires paid a bonus of 475,000 rupees (£35,625) and an annual rental of 95,000 rupees (£7125). Royalty payments, which were to be paid in Indian currency and not guaranteed in gold as they were in Iran, Iraq and Saudi Arabia, were at the rate of 3 rupees a ton, with a minimum guarantee of 250,000 rupees. This meant that, in the early years after oil was discovered, Kuwait's royalties averaged about 10 cents a barrel less than those of Iran, Iraq and Saudi Arabia. Moreover, Shaikh Ahmad was unaware that APOC and Gulf Oil, as part of their original agreement to combine forces in Kuwait, had decided that Kuwait oil should not be used to 'upset or injure' the marketing position of either 'directly or indirectly at any time or any place', that the two companies should 'confer regularly on this matter and have the right to require KOC to produce such quantities of crude oil as may be decided by the party making the request'. This only reflected the immense and growing power of the major oil companies, which for a few decades were able to control between them almost all the world's oil resources. The tiny state of Kuwait also had less bargaining power than its bigger neighbours Iraq, Persia and Saudi

Arabia, which might also have difficulty in standing up to the pressures of the Western powers but had more means at their disposal to resist them. There can be no doubt that Shaikh Ahmad's eleven-year struggle for an oil concession agreement which would balance Kuwait's immediate needs for an increase in income with its long-term interests was a triumph against formidable odds.

Although Shaikh Ahmad conducted these vital negotiations with the oil companies and the British government on Kuwait's behalf, with only the help of his close legal advisors, it would be quite wrong to suppose that he ran the shaikhdom as a simple autocracy and that he disregarded public opinion. In fact, the extreme authoritarianism of his grandfather, Mubarak the Great, was never allowed to be repeated. Ahmad's father, Jaber, and his uncle, Salem, who preceded him, had conciliated the merchants by sharply reducing the taxes and customs duties which Mubarak had imposed to finance his ambitious foreign policies. When Shaikh Salem died in 1921, the merchants and notables decided that they wanted formally to restore the situation to that which had existed before Mubarak's rule when they had an established role in government. Ahmad was outside Kuwait at the time, attempting to negotiate a truce with Ibn Saud.

Led by the writer and historian Yusuf al-Qinai, the leading citizens presented a series of proposals for political reform and the establishment of a consultative council (*majlis al-shura*). They nominated three members of al-Sabah, including Shaikh Ahmad, all of whom were sons or grandsons of Mubarak, and they proposed that the family should choose one of them as Amir. The choice fell on Ahmad, who accepted. In this way the principle was established that the succession was confined to Mubarak's descendants and that, while it was up to the Sabah family to choose the most qualified among them as Amir, public opinion had some influence in the matter. This was the system which had been applied before the bloody circumstances of Mubarak's accession and has worked smoothly ever since.

Shaikh Ahmad accepted the demand for a *majlis al-shura* but he did not agree to the notables' request that he should be its president, which would have made the council the effective government of the state. Ahmad and the Sabah family were not ready to share power to that extent.

A twelve-man council was formed (by appointment rather than election) – with six members from the eastern and six from the western part of the town – and a leading merchant, Hamad al-Saqr, became its president. Shaikh Ahmad consulted the council on all matters of importance, as he had undertaken to do, but since its members acted as individuals rather than representatives of groups or interests in Kuwaiti society their ability to influence the ruler was limited. The meetings of the council became increasingly rare and public interest declined.

This did not mean that the spirit which had led to the movement of 1921 disappeared. The pressure for representative institutions remained and in 1934, the year of the granting of the oil concession to KOC, a Kuwait municipal council was formed by election. Some two hundred electors chose twelve councillors by secret ballot from a single list – thereby establishing a democratic precedent in Arabia. The establishment of other elected councils followed – for education, for health and for *waqfs* (Islamic endowments). It was probably inevitable that the trend towards democracy was uneven. In 1938 the elected council for education fell into dispute with the Amir, who dissolved it and appointed another. When several members of the municipal council resigned in protest, he issued an amiri decree forbidding anyone to vote for them when they stood at the next municipal council elections. The ex-members of both councils then joined to form an opposition group known as the 'nationalist bloc', which produced a reform programme that was published in the Iraqi press. This included demands for more schools and hospitals, economic reforms and the closure of Kuwait to non-Arab immigrants and the encouragement of Arab immigration. Arab nationalism did not have to wait until the 1950s to plant itself in Kuwait. But when the British political agent made discreet inquiries about their intentions, the nationalists made clear that they were not aiming to change the rule of Kuwait but merely to introduce representative government.

The group had substantial support among the leading merchants such as the al-Ghanim and al-Saqr families and the most eminent notables such as the al-Adsanis, who had been the hereditary *qadis* (judges) in Kuwait for 150 years. Representatives of all of these in June 1938 presented a request to the ruler for the creation of a legislative council according to the hallowed tradition of *shura*, or consultation, from the Golden Age of Islam. They added the admission that 'the laxity shown by both sides has led to the neglect of this most fundamental principle'.

Shaikh Ahmad agreed. A committee of three eminent elders drew up a list of voters and elections were held to a fourteen-member council. The new council then elected as its president Shaikh Abdallah Salem al-Sabah, cousin of Shaikh Ahmad and son of his predecessor, Shaikh Salem. Abdullah al-Salem's acceptance of his election meant that the Sabah family was agreeing to a new experiment in the government of Kuwait. Shaikh Ahmad had refused the presidency of the 1921 council. The heir apparent's acceptance in 1938 gave the council much greater power. In fact, the legislative council's first law outlining its powers, which Shaikh Abdallah al-Salem persuaded the Amir to sign in July 1938, made the new parliament not only the sole source of legislative power but also the supreme executive power, since Article 5 declared that the president of the council represented the executive authority in the state.

The parliament at once made sweeping use of its new powers, appointing ministers of finance and defence, drastically cutting taxation and duties, taking over the duties of an appeal court, and purging corrupt officials from the police force and customs department. It opened three government schools, including one for girls (in addition to the two schools which already existed), and brought in more teachers from Palestine (the first batch having arrived in 1936). It also took steps to try to stop illegal immigration and made preparations to hold a census to establish what proportion of the population were long-standing Kuwaitis and how many had arrived since the First World War as 'mercenaries and refugees' – these were thought to make up nearly half the inhabitants.

However, like most idealistic reformers, the new council tried to move too fast. It took too little account of the delicate balance that existed in Kuwaiti society. Opposition grew not only among those whose vested interests or monopolies were affected by the reforms but among ordinary Kuwaitis, who objected to the invasion of the privacy of their families that the proposed census would involve. After the council had been in existence for six months, Shaikh Ahmad dissolved it. At first the members of the council tried to resist by shutting themselves up in the citadel with their police force. But their position was hopeless; they had lost control of the town and the armed beduin rallied to the ruler's support. With Shaikh Ahmad Abdullah al-Salem acting as mediator, they agreed to surrender. Shaikh Ahmad then proposed a new constitution. This cancelled the elected parliament and replaced it with another appointed advisory council, or *majlis al-shura*. It also re-emphasized the position of the amir as the supreme authority in the country whose person was to be 'protected and not touched'. He was to hold the position of commander-in-chief of the armed forces; appoint all senior officials and judges; declare martial law or states of emergency; conclude treaties and declare war. However, the draft constitution also laid down that there should be no distinction between Kuwaitis in matters of law, even if they were of different sects, and that Kuwaitis should enjoy personal liberty, their places of residence should not be interfered with and the right of ownership should be safeguarded.

The new council was shorn of any executive power. The amir would appoint its president. It shared legislative authority with the amir, who was also bound to consult it on all matters of importance. However, it was made clear that the amir made the ultimate decisions.

Not surprisingly, the elected members of the council rejected this

proposal, as it nullified their aim of representative government. Shaikh
Ahmad therefore went ahead and nominated an advisory council consisting of four members of his family and ten notables.

As had happened in the 1920s, this council gradually faded away. Its
meetings aroused little interest and were poorly attended. However, there is
no doubt at all that the events of 1938 had some permanent and positive
results. The short-lived council created an administrative framework of
government departments which survived and proved invaluable as Kuwait
entered a new and remarkable era of transformation.

4

The Challenge of Oil

Eighteen months after winning the Kuwait concession KOC spudded its first well at Bahra. It was dry. After another eighteen months, drilling was resumed in a different area – Burgan, some 28 miles south of Kuwait town, where the bitumen seepages had been observed in classical times. No one has ever discovered why the company chose to ignore such an obviously promising area for three years. In April 1938 oil spurted out from a well at enormous pressure. One of the biggest oilfields in the world – about 100 square miles in size – had been discovered. Its reserves were later estimated to be greater than those of the entire United States. Moreover, costs of production were low because the oil was relatively near the surface, at between 3500 and 5000 feet, and the average yield of each well at 5000 b.p.d. (barrels per day) compared with 250 b.p.d. in Venezuela and only 11 b.p.d. in the USA.

However, this did not mean that Kuwait's situation was immediately transformed. In 1938 total public revenues – mainly from customs duties and dues on the export of sand and pebbles to Abadan – amounted to 263,000 rupees or about £20,000. The oil company's rental payment added another £7125. The surplus after the payment of salaries to government officials amounted to a handsome £1700. When the British traveller Freya Stark spent some time in Kuwait in 1937 she felt detached from the world:

So perfect a small town, everything being right in the right surroundings, the lovely place and people . . . . I know of no place with such a charm of remoteness that is not yet solitude . . .

The first public notice to be posted by the Kuwait municipality gives a vivid impression of the condition and pace of life in Kuwait in the 1930s:

ANNOUNCEMENT

All inhabitants of Kuwait Town must comply with the terms of this notice; those who fail to do so will be liable to a fine.

First   Refuse and offal from houses must not be thrown into the streets but placed in the Municipality's refuse tanks or thrown into the sea or outside the town.

Second   Anyone who has an animal which dies in the house must throw it outside the town or in the sea and not on the shore.

Third   No one may spread stones or mud in the street for long periods. Those engaged in building are limited to the time of the work.

Fourth   No one may pour dirty water into the street or splash anyone who is passing.

Fifth   Anyone who wishes to build walls on the street must consult the Municipality.

Sixth   Bad meat, fish or vegetables may not enter the *suq* and any animal-fodder which has a bad smell must not be sold in the *suq* but on the beach outside the town.

Seventh Cars may not exceed a speed limit of 10 miles per hour in the town and 5 miles per hour in the *suq*.

Eighth   Package animals – strong horses and donkeys may not carry loads on their backs of more than two sacks of sugar and two cartons of rice and three *mannas* (a measure equivalent to 2 rotals) of dates. Weak animals must carry what they can bear.

Abdallah Jaber al-Sabah
Chairman of the Kuwaiti Municipality
17 Dhu 'l-Qa'da
[equivalent to 17 April 1930]

Lacking any sense of urgency, KOC did almost nothing to prepare for the outbreak of the Second World War. Production and export facilities had not been installed and these became impossible to obtain. Drilling continued until 1942 but the operations were shut down as a precautionary measure for the rest of the war. The British army was called in to plug the wells with cement.

However, the transformation of Kuwait into a major oil exporter started as soon as the war was over, and on 30 June 1946 Shaikh Ahmad ceremonially turned on the tap of the new pipeline at Burgan which took the oil to the shore and then by submarine hose to an offshore tanker. All the equipment still had to be laboriously brought ashore by lighter. But work began immediately on building a tanker-loading jetty – the largest in the world – and the new oil port named Mina al-Ahmadi after the ruler. This was completed in three years.

Exports rose from 800,000 tons in 1946 (earning revenues of £280,000) to 2.2 million tons in 1947, 6.4 million in 1948 and 12.4 million in 1949 – with revenues of £3 million. However, the rate of royalties paid by the company was still extremely low – even by the standards of the time. Between 1946 and 1949 they averaged 13 US cents a barrel – which was about 10 cents a barrel less than the rate paid to Iran, Iraq and Saudi Arabia because Kuwaiti royalties were paid in Indian rupees that were not guaranteed by gold. In 1949 the rate was reduced even further, to 9 cents a barrel, as a result of the devaluation of sterling.

Nevertheless, it was already apparent that Kuwait, with its tiny population, was destined for great wealth. It soon began to acquire a reputation as a new phenomenon – the oil city-state.

When Shaikh Ahmad died suddenly of a heart attack in February 1950 the metamorphosis had already begun. As Shaikh Ahmad had promised when he turned the tap to inaugurate the flow of oil, the new funds were used to improve the municipal services. The lack of water was the biggest problem of everyday life. The sweet-water wells at Jahra were insufficient to supply Kuwait City and until then drinking water had had to be brought in by ship from Iraq. The wealthier households might have a well in their yard which could be used for washing. The poorer inhabitants did their washing on the beach. Plans were laid for the only solution: sea-water distillation.

However, the real change in Kuwait's situation did not take place until after the accession of Shaikh Abdallah al-Salem on the death of Shaikh Ahmad. In the same year the aged but formidable King Ibn Saud of Saudi Arabia began asking why his kingdom was still getting only 21 cents a barrel from the Arabian–American Oil Company (Aramco) when Venezuela had passed a law in 1948 providing for a fifty-fifty share in oil profits between the oil companies and the government. Aramco's profits were approximately $1.10 per barrel. In Iran Prime Minister Mossadegh was demanding a similarly much improved deal from the Anglo-Iranian Oil Company. The US State Department was afraid of the growth of communist influence in the Middle East and aware of the need to conciliate the national governments in the region. The oil companies also realized that the situation could not remain unchanged. The Saudis had not yet gained much expertise in the oil industry but they were aware that Aramco was actually paying more in taxes to the US Treasury than to Saudi Arabia. In 1949 $43 million was paid in US taxes and $38 million to Saudi Arabia. As the Aramco chairman told a US congressional committee, the Saudis 'weren't a darn bit happy about that'. Aramco accordingly devised a scheme whereby additional payments to Saudi Arabia would be regarded as a foreign income tax, which meant that they would not be taxable in the United States. Saudi Arabia's oil revenues more than doubled as a consequence. It was not a genuine fifty-fifty division of profits, or anything like it, because it was left to the companies to decide what share of their total profits came from the oil production process and therefore had to be divided with the host government. On the other hand, the companies could argue that they alone and not the governments were bearing all the financial risks. But the enormous increase in oil revenues that followed the fifty-fifty agreements showed clearly how poorly the producing countries had been treated during the era of royalty payments.

For Kuwait the effect of the new contract was staggering because its royalty payments had been so much lower than those to other countries. On 29 December 1951 Shaikh Abdallah al-Salem issued Decree No. 5, applying the fifty-fifty principle to KOC. Oil output tripled between 1949 and 1952 but revenues increased twenty times, from £3 million to £60 million. The new concession agreement was extended for an additional seventeen years, to run until December 2026, and KOC was also granted offshore rights up to the limits of Kuwait's territorial waters. On the other hand, the revised agreement also included a provision for a further revision if more favourable terms were granted to any other Middle Eastern country.

Kuwait was fortunate once again in that the man who was ruler during the period of explosive and dangerous change was of exceptional quality. Closer to Shaikh Ahmad than to Mubarak the Great in temperament, Abdallah al-Salem gave an impression of thoughtful wisdom which was wholly genuine. A leading Kuwaiti historian described him when he was in his thirties as:

a generous and wise man with extraordinary intelligence and wit, who is a leading thinker and established poet . . . despite his youth, he is considered an authority on Kuwait's history.

He was held in respect and affection by such widely differing personalities as the senior British officials in the Gulf and President Nasser of Egypt. One of the former told me of his appearance of 'ponderous calm' as he considered a problem under discussion. Another has described his remarkably detailed knowledge of the tribal affairs of Yemen when civil war broke out in that distant part of Arabia. His frequent visits to India, which continued until the end of his life, gave him a wide view of the world and undoubtedly stimulated his belief in the need for political systems to evolve in the modern world. But, above all, his wisdom and unflappability were of enormous advantage as he presided over the modernizing revolution in Kuwait while ensuring that the country retained its identity. In that respect he had much in common with King Faisal of Saudi Arabia, who succeeded to the throne shortly before the death of Shaikh Abdallah.

Shaikh Abdallah had something else in common with his Saudi counterpart: he was extremely frugal in his personal tastes. At a time when some of the shaikhly princes of the Arabian Peninsula were beginning to become a byword for profligate personal extravagance, Shaikh Abdallah showed that he was prepared to devote much the greater part of Kuwait's oil revenues to the welfare of his people. This was a priceless political asset. There were countless stories about his parsimonious attitude in his private life. Towards the end of his reign he had some half a dozen comrades left with whom he enjoyed dining once a week. At first he invited them to his own modest palace, insisting that each of his guests provide their own contributions to the meal. Later, no doubt attracted by the current fashion for dining clubs, he arranged that the dinner should be held at the homes of each of his friends in rotation. When he inherited from his predecessor a large luxury yacht – a present from the oil company with gold fittings, including gold telephones – he promptly sold it to the Iraqi royal family and used the money to have a much more modest vessel built in a Kuwaiti shipyard.

In the early years of Shaikh Abdallah's reign Kuwait's oil revenues continued to rise astronomically. The huge increase which resulted from the introduction of fifty-fifty profit-sharing was reinforced by the crisis between Iran and the oil companies. In March 1951 the Iranian *majlis* voted to nationalize the oil industry in the face of what it regarded as APOC's refusal to give the government a sufficient increase in profits. The oil company, with the support of other major oil companies and Western governments, organized an international boycott of Iranian oil exports, and the Iranian oil industry came to a standstill. Kuwait was the main alternative source for the oil companies, and production was doubled between 1950 and 1952 to 37.6 million tons and increased further to 55 million tons by 1956. Kuwait was now the second largest exporter in the world after Venezuela and oil revenues rose from £60 million in 1952 to £100 million in 1957.

Shaikh Abdallah saw the priorities in Kuwait as water, health and education. Between 1951 and 1953 the pace of development was astonishing. Estimates were prepared for projects to be completed within five years costing £91.5 million. Apart from a water-distillation plant with an ultimate productive capacity of 5 million gallons a day and a power station of 75 megawatts, a lavish programme for building hospitals and schools was inaugurated. Plans were also laid for government buildings, a sewage system, a deep-water port and harbour, housing schemes, a natural-gas distribution system and a large new airport. However, a crisis soon developed which related to Britain's exploitation of its unique position in the Gulf. A development plan which was started in 1952 with a British director

was monopolized on British insistence by five British contracting firms, each
with a Kuwaiti partner. These were allowed to operate on a cost-plus basis
of 15 per cent of total expenditure. This application of the principle of British
exclusion of foreign competition from the Gulf and from the rich profits to be
made from Kuwait's oil aroused enormous resentment among Kuwaitis.
The Kuwaiti merchant mentality knew that the country was being stung.
In 1954 the British monopoly was ended; other European, American and
then Japanese firms entered the field and a trend was set which affected the
entire Gulf.

There can be no doubt that Britain's assumption of predominance in the
Gulf ultimately undermined its commercial position. Kuwaitis had always
driven British vehicles, and Britain's motor manufacturers took it for
granted this habit would continue. Starting from nothing, the Germans
broke into the market, offering to set up service depots, which the British
manufacturers had held to be commercially unjustifiable. As the number of
vehicles in Kuwait grew at an astronomical pace, there were more Mercedes
and Volkswagens to be seen on the roads than Austins or Vauxhalls.

The crisis caused by the excessive greed of the British contracting
companies was only brief and the transformation of Kuwait continued.

In 1936–37 there had been two primary schools in Kuwait; by 1947–48
there were nineteen, with 171 teachers of both sexes; but by 1958, when I
first visited the country, there were ninety-six government and private
schools with about 30,000 pupils (more than one-third of them girls), out of
a total population of 200,000. Secondary education for girls had been
started in 1951 and was rapidly expanding. Education accounted for about
10 per cent of the state budget. There were four hospitals and seventeen
clinics, with one doctor to every 1200 inhabitants. There was already a clear
distinction between the social standards of the youngest generation of
Kuwaitis pouring into their school playgrounds and their proud parents,
who had grown up in a much more austere atmosphere.

The most tangible change was in the provision of drinking water from the
first sea-water distillation plant, which opened in 1953. Until then sweet
water had been a luxury. Bathing and washing were performed with water
too brackish to form suds. There was a story, no doubt apocryphal, that oil
company officials shaved in gin. Many Kuwaitis were at first suspicious of
the distilled water, which seemed bland and lacking in body, and 5 per cent
brackish water was added to the desalinated sea water. The first desalination plant did not solve Kuwait's water problem. More plants had to be
built and it was some years before sweet water could be piped into every
home.

In no way was Kuwait City either comfortable or attractive in 1958. The old mud walls had been pulled down the previous year, and new suburbs were beginning to spread outside the old city boundaries and Fahad al-Salem Street, leading from the Jahra Gate to the post office, was taking shape as the main business thoroughfare. But the streets were potholed and partially unsurfaced; the newly imported consumer goods were thrown in random piles in the shop windows. There was no modern hotel because the government planned to build this itself and had prevented anyone else from doing so. The fortunate Western visitor stayed in the oil company guest flat. A year later a small and privately built hotel had opened on the seafront. It seemed luxurious, although the centrally controlled air conditioning was apparently uncontrollable: while the June temperature outside was 40 °C, the bedroom was so cold that I was obliged to use the rug from the floor as a blanket.

The temporary lack of social amenities was of secondary importance. In general Kuwait had made the right choices in giving priority to schools, hospitals, drinking water, sewerage and a modern port to accommodate the enormous boom in exports. The dispensing with the cost-plus principle for foreign contractors did not mean that all subsequent contracts were wisely allocated or that the right planning decisions were always taken. It is now acknowledged, for example, that far too little emphasis was placed on vocational training facilities for young Kuwaitis. But the great majority of the decisions proved to have been wise, and remarkably little of Kuwait's new wealth was wasted in view of the opportunities for useless extravagance that existed. Kuwait City, with its newly appointed development council, was in advance of other Middle Eastern capitals in the field of town planning, although admittedly the chances of implementing planning decisions were much greater than in ancient cities such as Damascus or Baghdad.

As I visited Kuwait at least once each year, I was able to observe the way it was growing. By 1961, when I went to write a survey of the now famous little oil state to mark its forthcoming independence, Kuwait City already appeared at night from the air as a huge metropolis, with the lights of the new suburbs stretching for miles into the surrounding desert. Some of the new villas were uncompromisingly garish but their gardens greatly improved the city's appearance. Palms, tamarisks and acacia (which were subsequently accused of causing hay fever) were being planted along the city streets and kept alive at considerable cost.

In that crucial decade before independence, Kuwait was undergoing changes more important than those to physical appearance. A profound shift was taking place in the structure and organization of its society, while at the same time it was beginning to play a role in the affairs of the whole region. In spite of Britain's theoretical control of Kuwait's foreign relations, the country was developing a distinctive foreign policy of its own.

One impact of the mounting oil revenues was to give economic as well as political power to the Sabah ruling family, and especially to the ruler. Hitherto – except for a period under Mubarak the Great – the weight of financial power had remained with the merchant class.

It was the Sabah family – and primarily Shaikh Abdallah himself – who decided how the oil revenues should be dispensed. Owing to his sound wisdom, about one-third was set aside for reserves for the future and most of the rest was used for building the infrastructure and creating a welfare state. This still left the problem of how the funds should be administered and how the increasingly complicated machinery of government should be organized. In the absence of any effective consultative council or parliament, legislative and executive powers lay with the ruler, who from time to time issued amiri decrees. With the advice of a special committee of prominent Kuwaitis and some other Arab experts, ten government departments were created which were the nucleus for the future government ministries, apart from foreign affairs, defence and information, which followed independence.

In 1959 the ruler appointed a Supreme Council consisting of the presidents of these departments as the highest advisory and decision-making body in the country. All of them were members of the Sabah family and each of them had the right to propose legislation on behalf of their departments. However, although they were paid princely salaries, the ruler's own share was modest in accordance with his own tastes. The Sabah family by no means monopolized the new prosperity. Apart from the spread of wealth through the generous welfare system, the state adopted a deliberate policy of buying land from private individuals at highly inflated prices which would then be used for development projects or resold to private buyers. This method of redistributing wealth through what might be called 'progressive negative taxation' (positive taxation having been virtually abolished) was necessarily somewhat crude. Later it would be criticized on the grounds that those who were already wealthy benefited most. For all that, it was quite as effective as the methods of income and capital redistribution in more developed economies.

After the appointment of the Supreme Council as the embryo of cabinet government, the ruler instituted a series of laws organizing the judicial and legal system to meet the demands of a rapidly modernizing and developing

Kuwaiti society. This included a new penal code, traffic law, maritime law, commercial companies law, labour law, nationality law, and so forth. The new organization of the judiciary law both simplified the system and gave the courts a greater degree of independence. Since 1925 there had been a political agency court established by the British to handle all cases involving non-Kuwaitis. Plans were made to abolish this on independence.

The task of developing within a few years a modern system of departmental cabinet government where none had existed was not easy. In 1961 Kuwait turned for assistance to the World Bank, whose mission reported that:

the principal weakness in the central government was a lack of unity and coordination. The authority of the Ruler was certainly all-embracing and this would have made for unity, had it not been that as a result of his exalted position and of the very limited capacity of his secretariat, he was rather isolated from the daily business of government and even from the policy-making centres in the agencies. Below his level of authority, the elements of unity and coordination weakened rapidly because of the principle of absolute equality among the members of the Supreme Council . . .

In fact the Amir rarely attended the weekly Supreme Council meetings, and in his absence no one acted as chairman. There was indeed absolute equality between each member of the Council. Such a democratic oligarchy could not function effectively, and the World Bank mission therefore recommended the appointment of a permanent chairman to act in effect as prime minister. This was the system that was adopted under the new constitution immediately after independence.

Apart from placing increased economic power in the hands of the Sabah family, the surge in development caused a rapid influx of population.

Construction and the rapidly expanding welfare services now created a new demand for both skilled and unskilled labour. The former were mainly northern Arabs – that is, Syrians, Lebanese, Egyptians and Palestinians – who came to man the schools and expanded government departments. The Palestinians formed the nucleus of what was to become the most substantial and affluent Palestinian community in any Arab state. The unskilled workers were mainly Iraqis and Iranians.

The first census, taken in 1957, showed a population of 206,473, of whom 45 per cent were expatriates. By 1960 the total population had risen to 321,621, of whom 49.6 per cent were non-Kuwaitis. This was a turning-point; since independence Kuwaitis have been a minority of the inhabitants of the country.

Between my first visit in 1958 and my second, during the prelude to independence, the increased presence of northern Arabs was striking. All the highest administrative and executive posts were reserved for Kuwaitis but, since the indigenous population lacked experience and training, most of the posts below the top levels were held by non-Kuwaiti Arabs. The merchant class were the best educated and the most administratively adept among the Kuwaitis and were therefore the most suited for high responsibility in the civil service. However, the merchants would not consider abandoning their private businesses at a time when their already substantial profits had every prospect of increasing. It was therefore normal practice for them to share their time between the public and private sectors. I discovered that it was usually easier to see senior Kuwaitis in their private commercial offices after 7.00 p.m. rather than in their government departments in the morning.

Such a system obviously carried the danger of widespread conflict of interests among Kuwaiti administrators, but at the time there was no real alternative. The problem could only be solved as the new generation of Kuwaitis with higher education and training appeared on the scene.

While accepting without question the need for non-Kuwaiti Arabs, the government's policy was always to maximize the number of Kuwaiti citizens in government employment. Former fishermen and pearl-divers, whose source of livelihood had been in decline for years, were recruited into the lower ranks of the civil service, while many of the beduin who had settled in camps outside the city walls helped to man the security services. As a result, although non-Kuwaitis formed a substantial majority of the total labour force in the country, Kuwaitis retained a small majority in the government service, which in itself accounted for about 40 per cent of total employment.

The beduin also found employment in the oilfields, and it was a conscious policy of the government to encourage them to settle in Kuwait City and incorporate them into the life of the state.

The settlement of several thousand beduin and the granting to them of Kuwaiti citizenship was significant but could not prevent the balance of population from swinging against the native Kuwaitis. The question of whether this development either could or should be prevented was frequently discussed in the first two decades after independence. There was the option of granting Kuwaiti nationality to all long-term immigrants who wanted it. This would have had the advantage of preserving a substantial majority of Kuwaiti citizens in the country. But I found that it was advocated only by a minority of pan-Arab idealists. Most Kuwaitis opposed the idea because they knew that it would speedily and inexorably change the character of the state; Kuwait's precious individuality would be lost. The second alternative was chosen. Under the Nationality Law of 1959, amended in 1960, Kuwaiti citizenship was confined to residents in Kuwait prior to 1920 and to their descendants in the male line and to foreign women upon marriage to Kuwaitis. Naturalization was made possible after a waiting period of ten years for Arabs or fifteen years for non-Arabs, and special exceptions were made whereby immediate citizenship could be granted to Arabs who had lived in the country since 1945 and had performed outstanding services to the country. But since only fifty individuals could be granted citizenship in any one year these provisions caused no marked shift in the balance of population.

While the government secured employment for as many Kuwaitis as possible in the public sector, it also set out to ensure that the private sector was not taken over by non-Kuwaitis. A series of measures laid down that all industrial firms must be 51 per cent Kuwaiti-owned and that non-Kuwaitis must have a Kuwaiti partner if they were to engage in business or own property in Kuwait. Banking and insurance were totally confined to Kuwaitis except for existing establishments.

If it had not been for the National and Commercial Companies Laws, Kuwait would surely have become a cosmopolitan society in Arab terms. As it was, the northern Arabs who provided most of the technical, professional and managerial skills in the early years remained almost entirely outside the social and political life of the country. Inevitably, they had some impact on the way in which the country developed because of the importance of the positions they held, but the essence of Kuwait remained unchanged. This wholly suited the largest single non-Kuwaiti Arab community – the Palestinians. The great majority of these had no desire for Kuwaiti citizenship, as this would have meant relinquishing their claim to their national identity and what they regard as their legitimate rights in Palestine.

So, although Kuwait was physically changing at an astonishing pace in the 1950s and an inexorable shift was taking place in its population structure, the country was far from losing its individual character. On the contrary, this character was becoming stronger and more self-confident.

For some two centuries Kuwait had enjoyed many of the attributes of an independent state. This was a result of a combination of factors, including its strategic position, the forceful personalities of the Sabah ruling family, the successful alliance between this family and the exceptionally able and dynamic Kuwaiti merchant class, and the skilful exploitation of rivalries between regional powers. However, until the discovery of oil, it had not seemed possible that Kuwait could aspire to full independence in the twentieth-century sense as a member of the Arab League and the United Nations. It would be the smallest UN member; and the difficulties of finding enough Kuwaitis to conduct the country's foreign policy were formidable – but they were no longer insurmountable. Ultimate separation had to come. Kuwait's achievement of financial independence through oil coincided with the powerful growth of pan-Arab nationalist sentiment, from which Kuwaitis were not immune. It no longer seemed acceptable to them that Kuwait's relations with the rest of the world, including those with their fellow Arabs, should be in Britain's hands.

These feelings were only intensified by the British–French–Israeli attack on Egypt in 1956. Abdul Nasser's action in nationalizing the Suez Canal Company had been immensely popular with most Arabs, and especially with the younger generation. Britain's action in attempting to reverse the situation by force in collusion with Israel and France, detested throughout the Arab World because of its ruthless efforts to suppress the Algerian revolution, caused an explosion of anti-British feeling.

The presence of Egyptian and Palestinian teachers in Kuwait and Cairo's Voice of the Arabs radio helped to sharpen the nationalism of the young Kuwaitis but they did not create the nationalist movement, as some of the British in the region (as well as the Eden government) professed to believe. The clubs which were becoming an important feature of Kuwait's political life declared their support for Nasser's Egypt and raised substantial sums of money to send to Cairo. When the Suez aggression took place, the oil company installations were severely damaged by sabotage. Crowds demonstrated in Kuwait City and outside the political agency.

The Kuwait government acted swiftly to contain the situation and no British individuals or property in Kuwait City were attacked. But the sentiments behind the demonstrations remained. Abdul Nasser's star in the Arab world continued to rise. The union of Syria and Egypt in the United Arab Republic in February 1958 aroused enormous enthusiasm as a prelude to a wider unity. When the pro-Western monarchy in Iraq, which had covertly sympathized with the British attack on Egypt in 1956, was swept away in a bloody revolution, few tears were shed in Kuwait, although Kuwait's elder statesmen had justified fears that the new republican regime in Iraq might press Iraq's long-standing claim to Kuwait.

The ruler and the Sabah family moved cautiously towards full independence. It was announced in Cairo in September 1958 that Kuwait had decided to become a member of the Arab League and to subscribe to the Arab League Development Bank. He also said that no Kuwaiti oil would be allowed to go to Israel and that strict measures were being taken to ensure that the oil companies conformed with the decision. In October 1958 the third Arab Boycott of Israel conference was held in Kuwait. As contacts between Kuwait and the independent Arab states multiplied, the Arab League invited Kuwait to take part in the meetings of the Arab League High Economic Council which were held in January 1959. Since the League's charter made independence an essential qualification for membership, the existing member states took steps to give the Economic Council a separate and independent status in order to allow Kuwait to join and take part in its activities.

Following the high tide of Nasserism in 1956–58 some opposition to Egyptian leadership was developing. Tunisia joined the League in 1958 but almost immediately withdrew, on the grounds that the organization was entirely dominated by Egypt. President Bourguiba considered Nasser's Egypt too radical and anti-Western. On the other hand, the radical new leader of the Iraqi republic, Abdul Karim Kassem, allied himself with the Iraqi communists and bitterly attacked Nasser from the left. In general, however, the division that developed in the Arab world was between radicals who followed Egypt's policy of positive neutrality – which in reality meant closer relations with the Soviet Union – and the conservatives, such as Jordan and Saudi Arabia, who remained deeply suspicious of the USSR and wanted to maintain their relations with the West. Even at this early stage Kuwait was starting to develop its own policy, which it has pursued doggedly ever since: positive neutrality or non-alignment towards the great powers and towards the Arab states. It could be said that among the Arabs Kuwait has been the most radical of the conservatives and the most conservative of the radicals.

The first reaction of the British government towards Kuwait's demands for independence was to suggest that the 1899 agreement should be amended, but by 1960 Kuwait was pressing for complete abrogation. Having absorbed at least some of the lessons of the Suez affair, the Macmillan government reached the conclusion that it would be better not to stand in the way of Kuwait's full independence and membership of the Arab League. Britain's primary interest was in Kuwaiti oil, which was regarded as one of the main pillars of sterling. As the Arab nationalist tide was still rising, it was felt in Whitehall, on the basis of advice from British officials in the Gulf, that this interest would be safest with a friendly but independent Kuwait.

In April 1961 the Indian rupee, until then Kuwait's legal tender, was replaced by a new currency, the Kuwaiti dinar; and on 19 June 1961 the ruler, Shaikh Abdallah, announced the termination of the 1899

Anglo-Kuwaiti agreement. According to letters exchanged on Kuwait's initiative, the agreement was cancelled as being 'inconsistent with the sovereignty and independence of Kuwait'. However, Britain expressed its readiness to come to the assistance of the government of Kuwait 'if the latter request such assistance'. The wisdom of concluding what amounted to a defence agreement with Britain after independence had been debated at length in the Supreme Council. It was certain to be attacked by Arab nationalists. But the Amir was convinced that Kuwait was unable to secure its own defences in the interim period until it could join the Arab League and the UN and establish regional alliances. In his address to the nation Shaikh Abdallah praised the existing close cooperation between the government 'as represented by officials from the ruling family' and the people and expressed his hope that this would continue. He also voiced the government's determination to strengthen the ties of friendship and brotherhood between Kuwait and the other Arab states.

It was not long before this determination was tested. The independent state of Iraq had never abandoned its claim to Kuwait, although under the pro-British Hashemite monarchy which ruled Iraq between 1921 and 1958 the claim was not pressed. Nuri al-Said, the wily Iraqi statesman who controlled the country's policies for much of this period, preferred to attempt to bring Kuwait within Iraq's orbit by drawing it into the pro-Western Baghdad Pact formed by Britain, Iraq, Iran, Turkey and Pakistan, and by offering to supply fresh water to Kuwait from the Shatt al-Arab. Despite the temptation to solve Kuwait's acute water problem, Shaikh Abdallah fended off these approaches. Such dependence on Iraq could be dangerous. Moreover, the Iraqi monarchy had been briefly ousted by a military coup in 1941 and this could happen again.

In fact it did occur again, in 1958. Nuri and most of the Iraqi royal family were murdered. Colonel Abdul Karim Kassem, a tall lean figure with staring eyes, became Iraq's nationalist military dictator. After a brief honeymoon period with the United Arab Republic of Egypt and Syria, he became a bitter enemy of President Nasser. When the pro-Nasser Arab nationalists in Iraq rebelled against him, he drew on the Iraqi communists for support. The two leaders exchanged insults, with Nasser calling him Kassem ('divider' in Arabic) of Iraq, and Kassem hurling back the bizarre epithet Nasser ('helper') of imperialism.

Kassem could not match Nasser's position in the Arab world despite Nasser's growing difficulties in Syria. But, as the leader of an important Arab country with great natural resources, he could make his challenge. Like Nasser, he used the Soviet Union's support to take his country out of the orbit of the West. Iraq's armed forces were being equipped with Soviet weapons and Soviet aid was helping to build a vital new port for Iraq on the Gulf at Umm Qasr, close to the Kuwaiti border.

Six days after the cancellation of the Anglo-Kuwaiti agreement Kassem made his move. At a special press conference he claimed erroneously that Kuwait had always been part of the province of Basra in the Ottoman empire, and consequently it now belonged to Iraq. He added that the Anglo-Kuwaiti agreement had been forged, and that Shaikh Abdallah should henceforth be regarded as the governor of the Kuwait district of Iraq.

The question at once arose: would Kassem invade? Kuwait's tiny army of 1500, with half a squadron of tanks and one battery of field artillery, was in no position to stop him. Yet the consensus of opinion, including that of British officials in Kuwait and Iraq, was that he would not. Certainly there was no prospect of any pro-Iraqi movement inside Kuwait. The 40,000 Iraqis working in Kuwait were mostly unskilled building workers who were satisfied with their high wages, while the non-Kuwaiti Arabs who did hold sensitive positions in the administration were mainly Palestinians,* Egyptians or Syrians, who had no desire to come under Iraqi rule. Saudi Arabia, Jordan and Egypt all expressed solidarity with Kuwait. Garrisoning a hostile Kuwaiti population supported by the rest of the Arab world would create endless problems for Iraq, and Kassem, although mercurial, could be rational in his strategic thinking.

However, no one could be sure. Intelligence reports of Iraqi troop movements helped to persuade Shaikh Abdallah to ask for British military support under the terms of the new Treaty of Friendship. There is no doubt that he did so without enthusiasm and there may well have been opposition from within the Sabah family. But it seemed to him a sensible precaution. There is equally no doubt that at least part of the British cabinet, supported by much of the British press, was only too pleased to be able to demonstrate that Britain was still capable of mounting such an operation in the aftermath of the Suez fiasco.

Within forty-eight hours the first British troops arrived – marine commandos from an aircraft carrier. Tanks from Bahrain followed, and troops by air and sea from Cyprus, Aden, Kenya and Salisbury Plain, until a force of 8000 men had been gathered.

A substantial body of British press correspondents was also in attendance, and I was among them. Attention was focused on the plight of the

---

*In a dispatch I wrote from Beirut on the subject to a leading London daily, a night sub-editor changed 'Palestinians' to 'Israelis', presumably on the grounds that Palestine no longer existed. My foreign editor was horrified but Kuwaiti friends, sensing what had happened, were amused.

British troops, who were mostly unprepared for camping in the desert at the height of the Kuwaiti summer, when daytime temperatures of 40 °C or more are normal and sandstorms are frequent. Several hundred of those who had arrived directly from Britain collapsed with heat-stroke.

I felt that it would be worthwhile using my Arabic to test the reactions of the Kuwaiti man-in-the-street to the crisis. The evening was the best time for this, when groups of Kuwaitis sat in the open air in the hope of attracting a cooling breeze. A series of conversations gave me the clear impression that, while most Kuwaitis were not opposed to the arrival of the British troops, they saw the best hope of warding off the Iraqi threat in the recognition of their independence by the other Arab states. Several of them criticized the other Arabs for the lack of firmness in their support. I cabled a cautious dispatch reflecting the results of my one-man poll.

At 2.00 a.m. the telephone rang in my hotel and I was informed that part of my cable was not being sent. The following morning a senior government official courteously explained that the decision had been taken at the highest level that the matter of Kuwaiti–Arab relations was too sensitive. I understood the reasons, although I was not pleased when a British Foreign Office spokesman lately warmly congratulated me on my dispatch, which was published and appeared to confine itself to the climatic problems of the British troops.

Kuwait moved swiftly to demonstrate that its independence was endorsed by the other Arabs. Within two months the British troops were replaced by a joint Arab League force from Saudi Arabia, Jordan, Sudan and the United Arab Republic. Although Kassem continued to threaten from time to time and British troops were again put on the alert during Christmas 1961, Shaikh Abdallah did not ask for their intervention. No one seriously believed that Iraq would now invade, even on the doubtful assumption that it had ever intended to. The Arab League force of 2000 men was only a token but it was sufficient.

During 1962 the Arab League force was gradually withdrawn and in February 1963, shortly after Abdul Karim Kassem had been overthrown and assassinated, the last Arab troops departed. On 7 May 1963 the United Nations Security Council approved Kuwait's application for membership, which had been vetoed twice since independence on the grounds that the new defence agreement with Britain left it under foreign domination. Finally, on 4 October 1963, the new Iraqi regime formally recognized the full independence and sovereignty of Kuwait in an agreement signed by both governments in Baghdad and diplomatic envoys between the two countries were exchanged a few weeks later.

5

The New Member

Some time before Kuwait achieved full independence and membership of the Arab League and United Nations, it had begun to shape a role for itself in the international community. It had already joined the economic institutions of the League. Immediately after independence, when the Iraqi crisis was in progress and Kuwait was trying to overcome opposition to its membership of the United Nations, it sent official emissaries to the Arab and African countries, to Asia and Latin America, to explain the Kuwaiti case. Throughout this period the Supreme Council was considering a major initiative which took the form of the establishment, on the last day of 1961, of the Kuwait Fund for Arab Economic Development. As its name implies, it was designed to provide soft loans for viable developmental projects in the Arab states. Later its scope was extended to include non-Arab developing countries.

Other Arab oil states later followed Kuwait's example but at the time it was a remarkable pioneering venture. In 1961 Kuwait was still a long way from fulfilling its own essential developmental needs, but here it was offering to share the good fortune of its oil revenues with its fellow Arabs. There was no doubt a strong element of shrewd calculation behind the move. In that era of radical pan-Arab nationalism there were numerous eloquent Arab spokesmen in Cairo, Damascus and Baghdad to put forward the view that Kuwait's oil wealth belonged by right to the whole Arab nation, and that it was the machinations of the imperialist powers which had left it in the hands of one small country. But at the same time there was a strong tradition in Kuwaiti society of helping those who were less fortunate or who had suffered disaster as the result, for example, of a bad pearling season. This principle was naturally applied to Kuwait's fellow Arabs – first to the small Gulf states which were still without oil and then further afield to Arab countries with urgent developmental needs such as Sudan and Tunisia.

The principal spirit behind the establishment of the fund was the present

Amir, Shaikh Jaber, who was minister of finance at the time. However, there can be no doubt that he had the full support of Shaikh Abdallah and his brother, Shaikh Sabah, who was prime minister and succeeded Shaikh Abdallah in 1965.

However, despite Shaikh Abdallah's concern with the Iraqi crisis and Kuwait's relations with the rest of the world, he lost no time in focusing his attention on the reform of Kuwait's internal system of government to meet the needs of an independent state in the 1960s. His first act after independence was to issue an Amiri decree calling for the election of a Constituent Assembly to draft a constitution.

An electoral law gave the right to vote to all Kuwaiti males over twenty-one years old, except naturalized Kuwaitis and members of the armed forces and police. A candidate had to be literate and over thirty years of age. Kuwait was divided into ten districts, with each district electing two representatives.

Elections were held in December 1961. The twenty who were successful out of seventy-three candidates represented the whole spectrum of Kuwaiti society – the leading merchant families, the beduin, the Shiite community and a small but active group of radical Arab nationalists.

The eleven members of the ruling Sabah family who were in the Council of Ministers joined the twenty elected members to form the full Constituent Assembly but they decided to abstain from voting on the constitution in order to leave this to the elected members.

In his law number 1, promulgated on 6 January 1962, the Amir outlined a system of government for the interim period until the permanent constitution came into effect. Its first article called upon the Constituent Assembly to draft a constitution to be based on 'democratic principles taken from the realities and objectives of Kuwait'.

The Constituent Assembly set up a five-member committee to draft the constitution with the assistance of an Egyptian legal expert. Working intensively to meet the twelve-month deadline set by the Amir, the committee produced a draft constitution of 186 articles for presentation to the Amir by 9 November 1962. Both the draft constitution and the debates upon it which followed in the Constituent Assembly showed a remarkable degree of political sophistication and realism, and ultimately of willingness to compromise to preserve the unity of the Kuwaiti state.

Compromise was required because, although the ruling family had clearly shown its willingness to abandon some of its traditional powers through the establishment of constitutional government, there were some members of the Constituent Assembly who wished to go to the lengths of turning Kuwait into a constitutional monarchy on a Western European model, with the freedom to establish political parties. It is clear that the great majority of Kuwaiti opinion did not regard such a system of government as suited to the realities of Kuwaiti society in the 1960s. On the other hand, there was a consensus both inside and outside the Constituent Assembly that government should be based on the principle of the separation of powers, including the independence of the judiciary guaranteed by law.

One important compromise concerned the nature of the Kuwaiti economy as described in article 3 of the draft constitution. Clearly it was not socialist but neither was it extreme *laissez-faire* capitalist, which would have been unsuited to Kuwait's closely knit society, nor state capitalist, which would have implied that all economic power should be placed in the hands of the government. The compromise that was reached described the national economy as 'based on social justice' and 'founded on fair cooperation between public and private activities' – the word 'fair' being added on the insistence of the merchants.

On the question of political parties the members of the Assembly were clearly influenced by the sad experience of other Arab states since their independence, where they had proved to be divisive and quite incapable of forming a basis of stable parliamentary life. For Kuwait with its small electorate they seemed even less appropriate. The draft constitution therefore only referred to 'freedom to form associations and unions'.

The constitution also represented a careful compromise between a presidential and a parliamentary system.

Legislative power was vested in the Amir and the cabinet. As head of state, the Amir's person was immune and inviolable and he would exercise his powers through his ministers, who reported to him.

It was his responsibility to declare a defensive war, offensive war being prohibited. He also had the right to initiate, sanction and promulgate laws.

However, no law could be promulgated unless it was first sanctioned by the Assembly. This was to be composed of fifty elected members – five from each of Kuwait's ten districts – and those ministers who had been appointed from outside parliament, provided they were no more than one-third of the number of elected members. (Ministers could, on the other hand, be appointed from among the elected members.) The Assembly had to approve all legislation and Assembly members had the right to initiate bills and question all ministers, who were made individually responsible to the National Assembly for the affairs of their ministries. Withdrawal of confidence from a minister required an absolute majority of the fifty elected members of the Assembly. The Assembly therefore had considerable powers.

The devising of the constitution required restraint on all sides. None of this would have been possible without Shaikh Abdallah's determination that a solution should be reached which, in the words of the preamble to the constitution, would produce a system in which 'the citizens are provided with more political freedom, equality and social justice'. When the constitutional committee reached deadlock in their discussions, they referred the problem to the Amir, who was able to use his influence to resolve it. This influence was based on the respect and trust he commanded.

One of the features of those years was the growth of a new element in Kuwaiti society – the trained professionals and administrators. A rapid expansion of the government bureaucracy was the inevitable result of the policy initiated by the Amir of using the oil revenues to provide advanced welfare services for the whole population. The civil service tripled in size in the first decade of independence. But it was also the government's aim to enable qualified Kuwaitis gradually to take over responsibility from the mainly Arab expatriates who were manning the administration. By 1973 there were some 35,000 Kuwaiti civil servants out of a total of nearly 90,000. The members of this new class were not as wealthy as the successful merchants but the more senior among them exercised considerable power and influence as administrators, teachers, engineers and lawyers. (There was an overlap in that some of the government administrators came from the prominent merchant families but the new class was nevertheless distinctive in character.) This new class showed increasing self-confidence and determination that it could have a share in the decisions which affected the way in which Kuwait was changing.

Elections to the first National Assembly were held in January 1962. Debates in the new parliament were vigorous. The majority of deputies were concerned with Kuwaiti social issues but there was a small radical Arab nationalist group who came to form something like an opposition and who constantly tried to divert parliament's attention to pan-Arab causes.

However, there were certain matters on which they all combined. These were the ending of the last formal ties with Britain, represented by the 1961 defence agreement and Kuwait's acquisition of control over its oil resources. On the first issue the government was in no hurry; it took the view that the treaty with Britain did not infringe Kuwait's sovereignty or allow it to interfere in Kuwait's internal affairs. But by 1968 the treaty was clearly superfluous. Kuwait's sovereignty and independence were universally respected and Britain had announced the complete withdrawal of all its forces from the Gulf by 1971. On 13 May 1968 the Kuwait government accordingly informed Britain of its intention to terminate the 1961 treaty 'in view of Kuwait's success in handling its international relations which renders the provisions of the treaty of 19 July 1961 unsuitable'.

On the second issue of gaining control over the country's major national resource there was no disagreement among Kuwaitis over the principle, only over the timing. Full control at that stage still seemed a distant goal. The major international oil companies were immensely powerful. Their scuppering of Iran's attempt to nationalize its oil in 1950 served as a warning against hasty action. Oil was being sold extremely cheaply and the governments of the producing countries were powerless to prevent it. Moreover, the price was falling. Kuwaiti crude was reduced from $1.72 a barrel in 1953 to $1.59 a barrel in 1960 and, although exports were increasing substantially, the revenues from the sale of what was not only Kuwait's major source of wealth but was also exhaustible were stagnant in the late 1950s. This was at a time when the prices of most other goods – and especially the kind of capital equipment that Kuwait needed for its development – were rising. Every Kuwaiti could understand what this meant.

The decision by the oil companies in August 1960 to cut prices further, after a series of cuts over the previous two years, provoked the creation of the Organization of Petroleum Exporting Countries (OPEC). Kuwait, which was still a year away from independence, was one of the five founder members, together with Saudi Arabia, Iran, Iraq and Venezuela, and has played a leading role in OPEC since its inception.

The declared aim of OPEC was to coordinate and unify its members' oil policies in order to oblige the companies to restore prices. It soon became apparent that the companies had no intention of doing this and there was no available means of forcing them. OPEC therefore turned its attention to obtaining an increased share of the profits per barrel from the sale of crude oil. To achieve this aim, OPEC's financial experts concentrated their attention on the new method of 'expensing' royalties, which meant that royalty payments (which were generally 12.5 per cent of the posted price – that is, the notional price by which payments were calculated) would no longer be credited against the 50 per cent income tax liability, as was the current practice in the Middle East, but treated as an item of the oil companies' costs.

The oil companies agreed to negotiate and eventually accepted the principle of expensing. However, they greatly reduced the potential value of the change by insisting on substantial discounts from the posted prices in calculating their income taxes. (Initially they proposed a 12.5 per cent discount, which would have nullified the benefit of the new system to the producing countries.) Kuwait agreed to an 8.5 per cent discount, to be reduced to 6.5 per cent in the following year. This would give Kuwait an additional income of 10 million Kuwaiti dinars for 1964, with larger increases in the following years.

When the government submitted the agreement to the National Assembly for ratification there was intense and vigorous opposition. Some deputies argued that they were being asked to rubber-stamp the agreement without time to study a complex matter which was vital to Kuwait's interests. Others pointed out that British Petroleum had recently accepted an agreement for North Sea oil with the British government which did not involve discounts.

This was the beginning of an era in which both radical and conservative deputies constantly urged the government to step up its pressure on the oil companies to increase not only Kuwait's share of profits from the sale of crude oil but also its control over the whole industry. The desire to increase revenues led on to the more important questions of direct Kuwaiti participation in all the processes of the oil industry, from production to refining and marketing, and the need to conserve the wasting asset of the country's major resource. To halt the flaring-off of natural gas and extend the lifetime of the oilfields by limiting output, the deputies constantly emphasized the need for a dynamic national oil policy.

The government had the same objectives as all patriotic Kuwaitis. Ministers often considered that the deputies' demands were excessive or premature and sometimes based on inadequate knowledge of the economics of the oil industry. They felt that they had achieved the best possible terms from the oil companies at that time on the basis of the bargaining strength of the two sides. During the 1960s and 1970s a formidable body of expertise in the oil industry was built up among Kuwaiti officials. In December 1965 the Ministry of Finance became the Ministry of Finance and Oil to highlight the fact that the government's financial policies were inextricably bound up with oil. But there can be no doubt that the constant pressure from deputies ultimately strengthened Kuwait's bargaining position vis-à-vis the oil companies and hastened the day when the country gained full control over its major national resource.

It was inevitable that Kuwait's infant democracy should suffer from growing pains which were at times severe.

The leading merchant families disliked the manner in which the new middle class were asserting the power and influence they had acquired.

Shaikh Jaber al-Ahmad al-Jaber al-Sabah –
Amir of Kuwait 1977–

Shaikh Saad al-Abdallah al-Salem al-
Sabah – Crown Prince and Prime Minister   1978–

Shaikh Ahmad al-Jaber al-Sabah – Amir
of Kuwait 1921–1950

Shaikh Abdallah al-Salem al-Sabah –
Amir of Kuwait 1950–1965

Shaikh Sabah Salem al-Sabah – Amir of
Kuwait 1965–1979

Shaikh Mubarak al-Sabah – Amir of
Kuwait 1896–1915

Top: Shaikh Salem al-Sabah visits Moscow as defence minister. Since independence Kuwait has maintained a non-aligned position

Above: Kuwaitis do national military service

Right: Kuwaitis prefer to live in houses with gardens than in tower blocks

Left: The suq in the 1950s

Below: A cafe in the 1940s

Bottom: The mud city wall was demolished in 1957

السَّابَات الجارية

CURRENT ACCOUNTS

حِسَابَات التوفير

SAVINGS ACCOUNTS

Above: New branches of banks are still multiplying

Below left: The nucleus of Kuwait University opened in 1966 – the first in the Gulf

Below right: A cafe today

The hand-plough (*below*) has disappeared, and pearling (*right and bottom*), once the basis of Kuwaiti prosperity, is almost extinct

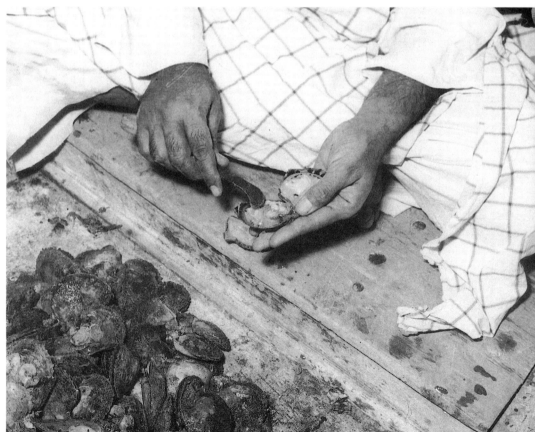

Traditional boat-building continues in Kuwait

The old port of Furdhah in the 1950s

Left: Intensive farming is the subject of constant experiment

Below: Solar power development is an activity of KISR (Kuwait Institute for Scientific Research)

Bottom: A supertanker at Mina Ahmadi oil port

Container trucks at Kuwait Port

A new chemical plant

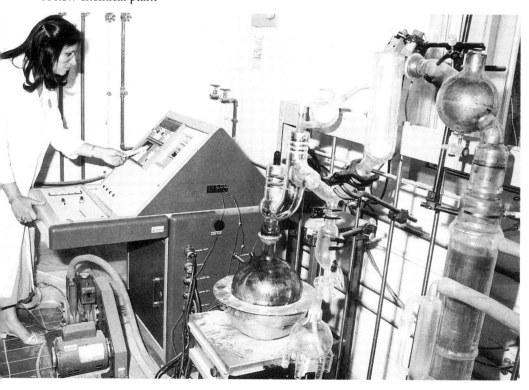

An increasing variety of recreations keep Kuwaitis active even in the summer months . . .

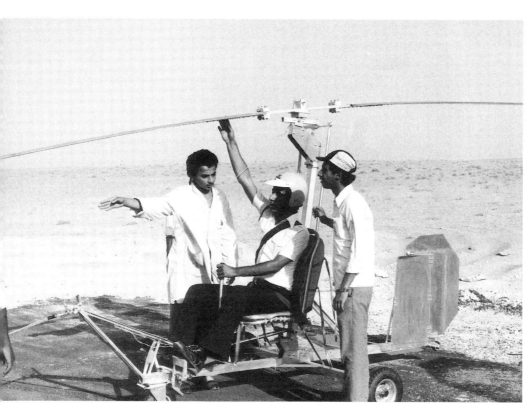

. . . their passion for football is well known

Left: Abdul Hussein Abdul Rida is an outstanding figure in the Kuwaiti theatre

Below: The Foreign Minister Shaikh Sabah al-Ahmad attends one of the many art exhibitions

Opposite above: The theatre is still lively and varied although some say its golden age has passed

Opposite below: The opera/oratorio/ballet on Kuwaiti themes is a popular form of entertainment

Attention is lavished on young children . . .

. . . including the handicapped

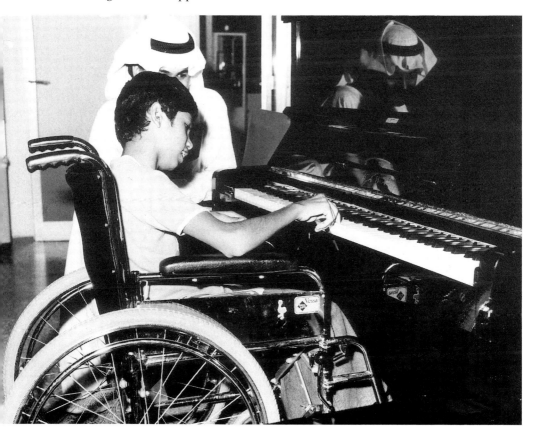

The award of outstanding degrees to university graduates by the Amir is an important event

More than half the graduates are girls

When the deputies of this class allied themselves with the beduin deputies, who generally represented the poorer sections of Kuwaiti society, they had a clear majority in parliament. One or two of the most prominent merchant deputies decided to give up parliamentary life. At the same time the small group of radical nationalists constantly tested the government's patience and the new democracy to the limit by the use of their freedoms under the constitution. A majority in parliament agreed with the government that there had to be more restraint.

The parliamentary crisis was briefly suspended when the much loved and revered Amir Abdallah Salem died on 23 Nobvember 1965 and was succeeded by his brother, Shaikh Salem al-Sabah, who at once formed a new cabinet under the new crown prince and prime minister, Shaikh Jaber al-Ahmad, Kuwait's present Amir.

Immediately afterwards the radical nationalist deputies resigned from the National Assembly en bloc. On a visit to Kuwait at the time I found that there was little public sympathy for their action, and even some of their supporters felt that it was the wrong way to protest. There was some apprehension about the consequences. The new National Assembly that was formed after fresh elections in January 1967 lacked both the experience and *gravitas* that had been provided by the leading merchants and the intellectual capacity of the radical nationalists. Deputies tended to devote themselves to the affairs and interests of the districts they represented and hardly any legislation of national importance was even discussed during the four-year life of the parliament. Without leadership or members of stature, the National Assembly declined in public regard. A feeling of malaise and concern with the country's political health spread through all sections of society.

Clearly, the situation could not be allowed to continue. In June 1970 the new crown prince and prime minister took the initiative by speaking directly to the people on radio and television.

It was a profound and thoughtful speech. He said that, after hearing many different views, he was convinced of the need for a firm domestic policy based on the country's experiences and circumstances. He said that the fact that the freedoms provided under the constitution had been unscrupulously exploited by certain people did not mean that the parliamentary system was unsound or unsuited to the present age but only that some had misunderstood it. He was especially critical of the Kuwaiti press for its unrestrained attacks on Kuwaiti individuals and leading figures in brother Arab states.

Shaikh Jaber gave a special warning about the excessive dependence on government spending and on employment in the state bureaucracy that had developed in the oil era and he called upon the private sector, 'which has not performed its duty properly', to invest more of the capital which it had placed abroad in national projects. He appealed to the merchants to resume their role in the political life of the country.

The response of the Kuwaiti public to Shaikh Jaber's move to reinvigorate the country's political life was generally favourable. The merchants showed that they were gratified by his appeal and ready to answer it.

A debate on the state of the nation was joined by all sections of society. In spite of complaints from the left that the government was limiting freedom of expression, the most conservative and the most radical views were aired. Islamic fundamentalists and Marxists wrote columns in the press – often in the same newspaper. Some sections of society – such as women and workers – had organized and were making themselves heard for the first time. The new women's associations welcomed the crown prince's speech as inaugurating a new era, but they also felt it was time for Kuwaiti women to be given the vote.

Kuwait had not yet found the right formula for its political institutions. But ten years after independence a political community was developing which showed remarkable signs of maturity. Criticism from some sectors of Kuwait's society and institutions was often sharp. Muslim militants felt that the nation was too secular and wanted a fully Islamic state while the left, whose views ranged between liberalism and marxism, seemed to want Kuwait to become a Scandinavian type of social democracy. But those who refused to accept the legitimacy of the Kuwaiti state and actively worked against it formed only a tiny minority. A fervent pan-Islamism or pan-Arabism was compatible with acceptance that an independent state of Kuwait was worth preserving because it could serve both causes.

The huge influx of non-Kuwaitis who were contributing to the country's development was a potential danger. The 1970 census showed that only 47 per cent of the population held Kuwaiti citizenship. But for several reasons this had not seriously threatened the stability of the state. The largest single group of immigrants were Palestinians. The small trickle who had entered the country in the 1930s became a flood after the Palestinians lost most of their country in 1948. A tiny minority who served Kuwait with special distinction acquired citizenship but their general wish was to remain Palestinian, even as exiles, rather than abandon their legal rights to return to their homeland. As the best educated and trained of the Arabs, many of them prospered in Kuwait and they had no motive to threaten the country's stability. Following the 1967 war and Israel's occupation of the rest of

Palestine, there was a new influx into Kuwait of some 200,000 Palestinians, most of them without employment. This was naturally a cause of concern and the government was forced to impose restrictions in March 1969.

After the Palestinians, the largest Arab group of immigrants was Egyptian, followed by Iraqis, Lebanese, Syrians, and others. They did not combine to form a single cohesive sector of the population. In the heyday of Nasserism many of the Egyptian teachers preached the doctrine of pan-Arabism, but since Nasser himself never aimed to subvert the Kuwaiti state this was not a danger. Among non-Arabs there were tens of thousands from the Indian subcontinent, who for the most part devoted themselves to sending home to their families as much of their pay as they could afford. They had no need to engage in politics.

A general election for the National Assembly's third term was held in February 1971. By general consent the election was free from government pressure. Ten members of the radical Arab Nationalist Movement were elected, who, together with six independents, formed an opposition inside parliament. The new Assembly was therefore more representative of Kuwaiti society than its predecessor. However, the leading merchants, who had welcomed the move to open a new chapter in Kuwait's political life, decided to abandon the legislature in order to concentrate on their traditional concerns of business. The leading merchant families were represented in parliament only by some of their younger members, who joined the opposition group.

The first decade of independence had provided Kuwaitis with invaluable experience in the management of the affairs of their small but complex and rapidly changing society. These were also the years when a distinctive Kuwaiti foreign policy developed.

6

Positively Neutral

On 21 December 1975 eleven OPEC oil ministers were meeting in the organization's Vienna secretariat when a terrorist gang headed by Carlos burst in to take them hostage. It later emerged that the gang was acting on behalf of the extreme left-wing Popular Front for the Liberation of Palestine. Carlos immediately set about dividing the ministers into two groups – the 'criminals', which meant the pro-Westerners, and the 'liberals', or anti-imperialists. In the first group were the ministers of Saudi Arabia, Iran, the United Arab Emirates and Qatar. The second included those of Iraq, Libya and Algeria. When Carlos encountered Kuwait's recently appointed oil minister, Abdul Muttalib al-Kazimi, he said: 'I don't know where to put you'.

This was a remarkable tribute to the role that Kuwait had carved out for itself in the world in the fourteen years since it had achieved independence. The claims of many Third World countries to be non-aligned with any power block were dubious and embarrassing. This was not true of Kuwait.

The term 'non-alignment' superseded 'positive neutralism'. Pandit Nehru, who in many respects was the founding father of the movement, preferred 'non-alignment', and it eventually became accepted. However, 'positive neutralism' was widely used in the Arab countries in the 1950s, and in Kuwait's case it had a real meaning. The state has endeavoured to remain neutral on all matters unrelated to Arabism and Islam, while it has vigorously promoted Arab and Islamic causes. It has refused to take sides in the numerous disputes between Arab states but has been tireless in its efforts to mediate. It was the first of the states in the Arabian Peninsula to establish diplomatic relations with the Soviet Union* but no one has ever suggested that it was moving into Moscow's orbit, although there was one

---

*Saudi Arabia had relations from 1927, but the Soviet Union closed its legation in Jeddah in 1938 and relations have not since been resumed.

hilarious occasion in November 1978, during an Egyptian press campaign against Kuwait as one of the leading critics of the Camp David agreements, when the loyally Sadatist Cairo daily *al-Akhbar* described the Kuwaiti Amir as: 'The new Marxist leader, Comrade Jaber Ahmad al-Sabah, President of the Soviet–Kuwaiti Party and Ruler of Kuwait.' The ludicrous charge merely served to demonstrate that Arab opposition to Camp David was not Soviet-inspired.

Given Kuwait's tiny population, combined with its ownership of some 10 per cent of the world's oil reserves, wealth was bound to be the main instrument of the country's foreign policy. But the instrument could not be effective without a coherent philosophy behind it. This philosophy developed very naturally from Kuwaiti traditions which had their roots in the time long before the discovery of oil. Kuwait then used its strategic position and relative prosperity in the region to preserve its independence. More powerful neighbours might covet the country but it was always preferable to the majority that Kuwait should retain its separate identity rather than be swallowed up by any one of them.

As we have seen, well before independence, when Kuwait officially acquired control over its foreign policy, the state had begun to examine carefully its role in the Gulf and the wider Arab world. In the 1950s Kuwait was regularly represented at meetings of the organs of the Arab League. As early as 1954, Shaikh Abdallah paid for the construction and running of schools in the Trucial States of the lower Gulf such as Abu Dhabi, Dubai and Sharjah (now the United Arab Emirates), where oil was still to be discovered and local British officials had been able to squeeze only very small sums out of the British government for development.

The establishment of KFAED – the Kuwait Fund for Arab Economic Development – on 31 December 1961, the last day of Kuwait's first full year of independence, provided a formal basis for a major aspect of Kuwait's relationship with its fellow Arabs.

KFAED was a remarkable institution in a number of ways. It was the first agency of a national government – as opposed to an international agency – created for the specific purpose of regional development, and it was the first case of a non-industrialized country providing aid to the developing world. Other Arab oil states have since followed the example but Kuwait was the pioneer.

There were two other striking aspects of the fund. One was its high degree of independence and the other, wholly characteristic of Kuwait, was its neutrality towards the political and economic systems of the recipient countries. Although it was naturally financed from government revenues –

with an original authorized capital of 50 million Kuwaiti dinars (£58 million), which was doubled in 1963 and again in 1966 – and the impetus came from the ruling family, especially Shaikh Jaber, who was then Minister of Finance, in practice the board of directors and the director-general had decisive control over the fund's policies. The board consisted of 'eight competent Kuwaitis' appointed by the minister of finance and oil, who was its ex-officio chairman. The board appointed the director-general. The first was Abdul Aziz al-Bahr, who in 1963 was succeeded by his assistant, an outstanding member of Kuwait's new technocratic elite, the twenty-seven-year-old Abdul Latif al-Hamad. Educated at Claremont College and Harvard in the USA, and a lover of Western classical music, al-Hamad is the kind of Kuwaiti who can absorb what the West has to offer without any damage to his Arab identity. Fortunately, such people are far from rare.

Starting operations in a single room without a secretary, the fund built up a staff of Arab specialists from a dozen countries. In time it was possible to recruit more young Kuwaiti graduates but a full-scale process of 'Kuwaitization' (or *takweet*, in the less clumsy Arabic term) was never thought necessary in what was essentially a pan-Arab institution.

Abdul Latif al-Hamad, who did much to mould the character of the fund, was instinctively in harmony with the underlying principles of Kuwait's foreign policy. The granting of development loans to Arab countries was not affected by the political orientation of their regimes or their social and economic policies.

In the 1960s Egypt was growing increasingly socialist, Lebanon was *laissez-faire* capitalist, Tunisia was mildly socialist but pro-Western, while Sudan swung between military and parliamentary regimes. All of them received substantial loans from the fund. This did not mean that there was no regard for the economic viability of the projects for which the loans were requested. On the contrary, the fund's growing team of experts examined all the implications of each project with care. From its early days KFAED also offered technical assistance such as the conduct of feasibility studies. The Arab nature of the fund made it easier to place special emphasis on the human factor in other Arab countries. But the fund's criteria were less purely economic than those of most international development agencies and they were certainly not related to any capitalist or socialist theory. The fund administrators were always prepared to look at long-term social benefits, even when the economic return was likely to be low. They enjoyed the enormous advantage that they were Arab economists or specialists dealing with Arab societies.

The result was that KFAED began to step in where the World Bank had refused, or was hesitating, to go. The World Bank had originally agreed to finance a vital electrification scheme in Tunisia but had withdrawn because of unsettled problems between Tunisia and French electricity companies which had been nationalized. With no such inhibitions KFAED took the place of the World Bank. Another farming development scheme in Tunisia had been turned down by the World Bank because the bank had felt that its profitability was too low. Again the Kuwaiti fund stepped in.

The Kuwaiti fund has not suffered from the same drawback as most national aid organizations, which is that as a matter of national interest the donor countries tie their development aid to their own goods and equipment. This reduces the value of the loan to the recipient countries and sometimes causes resentment. Since Kuwait does not manufacture capital goods, KFAED does not make any such requirement. However, it would be absurd to suggest that the fund is immune from government pressures. It cannot be because it is seen by the outside word as a major aspect of Kuwait's character. Whatever the fund does is considered to be government policy.

The fund faced a challenging test early in its history. In 1963 a mission from the newly independent government of Algeria arrived in Kuwait on a tour in search of aid. After their seven years' struggle for freedom from French colonial rule, the Algerians enjoyed enormous prestige in the Arab world. The Kuwait foreign ministry was anxious to announce an immediate substantial loan as a signal of Kuwait's regard, but this would have allowed no time to study the projects for which it was to be used. The fund was able to secure a compromise whereby an immediate loan of £10 million was announced but was made subject to subsequent agreement on its use. As the fund became better established and its prestige grew, its independence became more assured. This trend was not diminished but enhanced when Shaikh Jaber succeeded as ruler at the end of 1977. He made no attempt to subject the fund's activities to state policy.

In 1974, following the quadrupling of oil prices and the huge increase in Kuwait's revenues, KFAED began a new policy of extending loans to non-Arab countries as well as to the Arab states. KFAED was no longer a purely Arab fund, although it retained its original name. It was not difficult for the fund to adapt the experience and expertise it had built up to non-Arab countries.

However great the role of the fund in the newly independent Kuwait in the 1960s, no one in the government was under any illusion that it would fulfil all the country's responsibilities towards the rest of the world and to the Arab countries in particular. After the fall in 1963 of Abdul Karim Kassem, the ruler of Iraq who had laid claims to Kuwait, the new Iraqi government recognized Kuwait's independence and Kuwait made Iraq a loan of $84 million, which was in fact a gift, out of its reserves. Similar gifts followed to other important Arab countries such as Syria and Egypt. Cynics maintained that Kuwait was simply paying heavy premiums on an insurance policy for its sovereignty and independence, and in the case of Iraq this was at least partially correct. But Kuwait also indubitably saw itself as strengthening the Arab countries which were bearing the military brunt in the struggle against Israel.

In January 1964 President Nasser of Egypt called a meeting of Arab heads of state in Cairo – the first of the Arab summit conferences. The immediate pretext was that Israel was planning to divert some of the waters of the river Jordan from the few miles it ran through Israel to the Negev Desert. This was something that the Arab front-line states had repeatedly sworn to prevent. But Nasser was also concerned that the hot-headed young Baathist regime in Damascus would launch some action against Israel which would plunge the Arabs into a war for which they were not prepared. The Arab world was in disarray. Nasser's Egypt remained the single predominant force but its leadership was challenged by Syria, which had seceded from the United Arab Republic a year earlier, and by Saudi Arabia, with which Egypt was in dispute over the royalist/republican civil war in North Yemen. Faisal of Saudi Arabia, crown prince and shortly to become king on the abdication of his brother Saud, was then the rising star in the Arab world. But it was the presence of Shaikh Abdallah al-Salem, the Amir of Kuwait, who was then in the last year of his life, which evidently helped to hold together the Cairo conference and the second Arab summit which followed in Alexandria in September. The affection and respect with which he was greeted by his fellow heads of state was apparent to all those who attended.

The two summit conferences took various decisions to strengthen the Arab front with Israel. There was to be a new Palestinian military force – the Palestine Liberation Army – a substantial subsidy to the Jordanian armed forces and a fund for the diversion of the sources of the Jordan in Lebanese and Syrian territory before they entered Israel. Kuwait made the largest contributions for all these purposes. In the event the apparent rapprochement achieved between the Arab states was neither sustained nor solid. The United Arab Military Command which had been established was ineffective because of mistrust between the allies, and a series of political blunders led to Israel's pre-emptive strike against Egypt in June 1967. Instead of fighting Egypt, Syria and Jordan simultaneously, Israel turned the weight of its forces against each in turn. The units of the Palestinian Liberation Army which had been trained were scarcely engaged in the brief conflict.

Certainly none of this was the fault of Kuwait, which had exerted all its efforts towards reconciliation between the Arabs. After the disaster the new Amir, Shaikh Sabah Salem, attended the Arab summit held in Khartoum at the end of August to discuss the consequences. Only the embittered Syrian regime refused to attend. The unanimous decision of the heads of state was to refuse any negotiation while the Arabs were in such a state of weakness. The three states which at that time had substantial oil revenues – Kuwait, Saudi Arabia and Libya – agreed to help Egypt and Jordan rebuild their economies and restore their shattered military machines. The summit decided that Egypt should be paid £95 million a year and Jordan £40 million 'until the traces of aggression are removed'. Of this total of £135 million, Kuwait contributed £55 million, Saudi Arabia £50 million and Libya £30 million.

While Saudi Arabia's oil reserves were much greater than those of Kuwait (about 25 per cent of those of the non-communist world as compared with Kuwait's 10 per cent), Saudi Arabia's much greater population and developmental needs meant that Kuwait could afford to make the larger contribution, although with its total revenues still slightly below £250 million this involved considerable sacrifice for Kuwait and the postponement of some cherished developmental projects. The money came partly from state reserves and partly from the general budget.

Kuwait continued the payments and even increased those to Egypt. However, in 1971, following the brief but bloody Palestinian/Jordanian civil war and the subsequent expulsion of all the Palestine Liberation Organization fighters from Jordanian territory, the Kuwait government, with vigorous support from the National Assembly, cut off the subsidy to Jordan to express its disapproval of Jordan's action. The Amir of Kuwait took part in the emergency summit called by President Nasser in Cairo when the civil war was at its height in order to bring King Hussein and Yasser Arafat face to face and halt the fighting. At the end of the summit the exhausted Nasser bade farewell to the Amir at Cairo airport and went home to die of heart failure. The heads of state hoped and believed that a compromise had been achieved, but this broke down in the following year. The last Palestinian guerrillas were driven out of Jordan and some were even forced to take refuge across the Jordan river in Israeli-occupied territory. Outrage at this event, which was a humiliation for all the Arabs, caused Kuwait to cut all its aid to Jordan and at the same time to make a substantial grant to the PLO. The aid to Jordan was restored only after the 1973 war, when Arab differences were temporarily resolved and Jordan contributed to the struggle with Israel by sending troops to fight alongside the Syrians.

Kuwaiti actions of this kind are sometimes attributed to the large number of Palestinians in Kuwait, which today may constitute nearly 20 per cent of the population. It would be absurd to suggest that the Palestinian community, who play a crucial role as teachers, journalists and administrators, have no influence on the climate of political opinion in Kuwait. But anyone who knows Kuwait is aware that the mainsprings of political attitudes lie within Kuwaiti society. Kuwaitis understandably believe that their interests should have priority inside the country; only a few ultra-idealists would hold that other Arabs should have exactly the same rights as Kuwaiti citizens. But a belief in 'Kuwaitization' of the country's institutions wherever and whenever possible by no means implies isolationism. The great majority of Kuwaitis, from radical and secular pan-Arabists through moderates and conservatives to Islamic fundamentalists, are happy to see their country adopt a vigorous and distinctive foreign policy. The Palestinian question is normally something on which they all can agree.

A national consensus has grown up around a belief that Kuwait should be in the vanguard on two issues: the promotion of Arab and Islamic unity, and the independence of the Arab Gulf region from great power influence and control.

One reason why Kuwait's foreign policy has shown such remarkable consistency since independence is that for nearly all this time the same man has been in charge. Shaikh Sabah al-Ahmad, a brother of the present Amir, became foreign minister in 1963; and when Andrei Gromyko left the Soviet foreign ministry to become prime minister in 1985, Shaikh Sabah became the longest-serving foreign minister in the world. The skill, courtesy and humour with which he fielded the questions of journalists from some eighty nations at the end of the Islamic summit conference in Kuwait in January 1987 demonstrated his combination of national diplomatic ability and immense experience. He is generally suave but not always. One of his first diplomatic missions was to Tokyo in 1964. Without hydrocarbon resources, Japan was increasing its stake in Arab oil and expanding its business relations with the Gulf. The Kuwait government felt that Japan should take an interest in Arab political concerns and Shaikh Sabah al-Ahmad went to Tokyo to explain the Arab view of the Palestinian question. When he thought that the Japanese government was showing indifference, he reacted sharply. The Kuwaiti press backed him up by demanding that all Japanese interests in Kuwait be liquidated. The Japanese government apologized and the incident was considered closed; but a lesson had been learned.

Kuwait has always been ready to mediate between the Arab states. Saudi Arabia, as the major regional power, with its unique prestige at the heart of the Islamic world, has also played a mediating role – especially since the death of President Nasser in 1970 meant that the Kingdom was no longer regarded as the leader of one of the two rival Arab camps. But Kuwait has often been able to make a special contribution. In August 1966 it even made a brave but unsuccessful attempt to mediate between Egypt and Saudi Arabia in their bitter dispute over Yemen.

When the civil war between royalists and republicans ended in 1969 with a compromise, Kuwait cultivated its relations with the Yemen Arab Republic of North Yemen and provided it with substantial aid. The government in Sanaa was happy not to have to rely solely on Saudi Arabian assistance. On the other hand, Kuwait also developed its ties with the People's Democratic Republic in South Yemen, which succeeded the British departure in 1967. The PDRY was moving steadily leftwards to become the first semi-Marxist state in the Arab world. Saudi Arabia refused to recognize the Aden regime but the Kuwaiti view was that a boycott was not the best way to prevent the PDRY from moving entirely into the communist orbit. It provided the PDRY with aid which matched its aid to the North. In July 1978, when most Arab states expressed outrage at what they believed was the PDRY's complicity in the assassination of North Yemen's President Ghashmi, and an Arab League decision was taken to freeze political and economic relations with Aden, Kuwait said it would abide by the decision but refused to close the South Yemeni mission in Kuwait. This placed Kuwait in a unique position to mediate between the two Yemens when fighting broke out between them in 1979, and between the sultanate of Oman and the PDRY, which had been supporting a smouldering rebellion against the sultan's government in Oman's southern Dhofar province. It was largely through Kuwait's efforts that Oman and the PDRY agreed to cease hostilities and establish diplomatic relations in October 1981.

When Britain suddenly and unexpectedly announced its complete withdrawal from the Gulf by 1971, Kuwait was concerned about the future of the lower Gulf. The Kuwaitis themselves had ceased to regard the British presence as a protection for their independence, but Bahrain, Qatar and the seven even smaller states of the Trucial Coast still felt that they depended on British guarantees. Iran laid claim to Bahrain and to certain offshore islands at the southern end of the Gulf. Since the smaller shaikhdoms could hardly sustain the status of full independence and membership of the UN, the obvious solution was for them to form a union or federation. From the outset Kuwait and Saudi Arabia supported the concept of a federation of the nine.

However, there were enormous problems. The ruling families of the shaikhdoms were proud of their independence and reluctant to give up any of their sovereignty even if they saw it was necessary. There were dynastic rivalries between some of them, and there was the special problem that Bahrain would tend to dominate any federal structure in which power was shared on the basis of population. Some of the rulers even asked Kuwait to join the federation and provide the site of its capital in order to counterbalance Bahrain. Kuwait declined but did everything to encourage the negotiations. When these seemed to be getting nowhere after two years, the foreign minister, Shaikh Sabah Ahmad, joined Prince Nawwaf of Saudi Arabia in a delegation which toured the lower Gulf in January 1971 to try to break the stalemate. A second mission headed by senior diplomats followed. Bahrain and Qatar helped towards a solution by opting for full independence, and on 18 July six of the Trucial States (with only Ras al-Khaimah temporarily refusing to subscribe) announced the formation of the United Arab Emirates. It was a triumph for the political foresight of the Arab Gulf shaikhdoms to which Kuwait, with its decade of experience of independence, made a valuable contribution.

For the past twenty-five years the Kuwait government has been fully consistent in its policy of rejecting any notion of foreign military bases in the Arab Gulf region or of tying itself to outside powers in a military pact. While avoiding the extreme anti-Western rhetoric of the most radical Arab states, it has often been harshly critical of the Western powers, and especially of the United States for its unmitigated support of Israel. As with the country's support for the Palestinian cause and the PLO since its rise to prominence in the wake of the 1967 Arab–Israeli War, this tendency to take an anti-Western stand is sometimes attributed to the Palestinian presence in Kuwait. But in fact it is a wholly characteristic expression of the Kuwaiti personality.

In 1963, when Kuwait became the first of the Arab Gulf states to establish diplomatic relations with Moscow, the gesture was startling. The Soviets were at first inclined to be patronizing because they felt Kuwait was still politically and militarily dependent on Britain and economically controlled by the oil companies. They also believed that Kuwait's ruling family would soon be swept aside. Khrushchev showed his ignorance in a speech in Cairo in May 1964, when in a highly personalized and insulting attack he accused Kuwait's Amir of selfish extravagance in the spending of his people's wealth. A more ludicrous description of the ascetic and humanitarian Abdallah al-Salem would be hard to imagine.

Gradually the Soviet Union's view began to change as it was forced to accept that Kuwait's non-alignment was genuine. A delegation of the Supreme Soviet to Kuwait in March 1974 praised its policy of non-alignment and refusal to join military pacts and declared that Kuwait's views on most international problems were similar to those of the USSR. At the time Soviet Arab experts were still analysing Kuwaiti society in Marxist terms. They saw the immigrant workers as the potential leaders of the class struggle which could only be temporarily arrested by the bourgeois welfare state policies of the Kuwaiti government. By the 1980s the Islamic revolution in Iran required a further reassessment. If there was a threat to Kuwait's stability, it was not from a proletarian uprising but from Islamic fundamentalism. The Soviets seem to have accepted that the existing regimes in the Arab Gulf states are preferable to any likely alternative. They began a policy aimed at reassuring the Gulf states about their intentions with a denial that the close Soviet ties with the semi-Marxist regime in the People's Democratic Republic of Yemen constituted a threat. This resulted in the establishment of diplomatic relations between Moscow and the UAE in 1985. Kuwait was no longer the only diplomatic channel between the region and Moscow but it had been so for more than two decades and during that time it had provided a useful service to all its brother regimes in the Gulf.

7

The Economic Adventure

The discovery of oil has been changing the lives of Kuwaitis for no more than a single generation. Yet the change has been far more than superficial. It is not only that real poverty has been eliminated and affluence has become the norm, to the extent that a Kuwaiti millionaire is someone of modest means; despite the vigorous survival of traditional social values, the Kuwaiti outlook on the rest of the world has been transformed. Kuwait's new place in the world is taken for granted by its people.

During the first half of the period since the influx of oil revenues began, the government's attention was devoted to providing the Kuwaitis with the services of which most of them had been deprived – piped water, electricity, modern housing, schools and hospitals – as well as the infrastructure of ports, airports and paved roads. As we have seen, the government's concerns were far from entirely insular. Much of the new wealth was either given or loaned on easy terms to other Arab states which were less fortunate. As the oil revenues increased steadily by about 10 per cent each year (from £100.3 in 1955 to £216.1 in 1965, the year that Shaikh Abdallah Salem died), there was little thought at that stage about the future or, in simple terms, about what would happen when 'the oil ran out'.

From 1968 onwards, however, Kuwait was aiming to secure 'reasonable participation' in the ownership of the Kuwait Oil Company. This was part of a common OPEC policy, one of the prime objectives of which was to secure some control over the rate at which the countries' major but exhaustible resource was used up. Saudi Arabia led the negotiations with all the oil companies operating in the Gulf on behalf of Kuwait, Bahrain and the UAE as well as itself and, by October 1972, after tough and lengthy discussions, an agreement was reached providing for an initial government participation of 25 per cent in the concessions of the respective oil companies in each country to rise very gradually until it reached 51 per cent by 1982.

In 1971 the Kuwait government was also making plans for a joint venture between its own Kuwait National Petroleum Corporation and BP and Gulf Oil, the parent companies of KOC, for the exploitation of Kuwait's natural gas.

As soon as the third Kuwait National Assembly was elected in February 1971, it began to press for the acceleration of Kuwait's acquisition of 100 per cent control over its hydrocarbons. One of the points made by the deputies was that for over a quarter of a century the companies had continued to burn off the natural gas, although they knew very well, while Kuwaitis were unaware, that this was against the law in the United States. Partly as a result of this pressure, the government demanded, and a year later secured, the right to acquire any amount of natural gas produced in association with crude oil within the KOC concession area.

The National Assembly then turned its attention to the participation agreement. Deputies argued that the pace was far too slow. Some claimed that the companies owed Kuwait compensation for the minute royalties they had paid and for their unilateral decision to reduce prices when everything was under their control. The Assembly refused to ratify the agreement and the government agreed to reconsider it. Fortified by the fact that other Arab countries such as Libya and Algeria had unilaterally secured over 50 per cent participation, and the big shift in power towards the oil-producing countries which resulted from the 1973 Middle East war, Kuwait was able to secure 100 per cent or a complete takeover in December 1975.

An attempt to prevent the early exhaustion of the country's oil reserves did not have to wait for the takeover of KOC. In February 1972 one deputy claimed that the reserves had been vastly overestimated and would be exhausted in twelve years rather than seventy as the oil companies were saying. The government denied this but it did instruct KOC to limit output to its current level of 3 million b.p.d., instead of increasing it annually by 5 per cent as had previously been intended. This ceiling was later reduced to 2 million b.p.d., then to 1.5 million in 1980, and 1.25 million in 1983. With the huge oil-price rises of the 1970s Kuwait could restrict production and still enjoy increased revenues. When the oil recession came in the 1980s production had to be restricted to Kuwait's OPEC quota. Revenues fell sharply but by then the country's economic infrastructure had been completed and its needs were reduced. Since proved reserves had increased from 66 billion barrels to 90 billion, their life expectancy could be estimated at 240 years at current rates of production. This was vastly different from the prospect that the country might 'run out of oil' before the middle of the next century.

Five years after the nationalization of 1975 the government reorganized the industry under a new Kuwait Petroleum Corporation which directly controlled five major subsidiaries: the old KOC, which is responsible for crude oil and gas production; the Kuwait National Petroleum Corporation (KNPC), which controls refining, gas processing and product marketing; the Petrochemical Industries Company (PIC), which manages domestic petrochemical and fertilizer production; the Kuwait Oil Tanker Company (KOTC), which is responsible for the transport of crude oil and liquified petroleum gas (LPG) and the Kuwait Foreign Petroleum Exploration Company (Kufpec), which undertakes oil and gas exploration in overseas concessions.

KPC has become the eighth and youngest sister of the giant US, British, Dutch and French international oil companies, who were christened "the Seven Sisters" in the 1950s by the head of the Italian state oil industry, Enrico Mattei. It conducts a worldwide network of operations which stretch from the well-head to petrol pumps and factories.

KPC began purchasing overseas interests in 1981, when it acquired the US oil engineering and exploration firm Santa Fe International. During the 1980s Santa Fe and Kufpec extended their operations to search for oil and gas throughout most of the globe, with Santa Fe concentrating on the American continent and Kufpec on Africa, the Middle East, Asia and the Pacific region. In 1990 Kufpec has some 30 joint ventures or is acting as operator for concessions in the Soviet Union, China, Indonesia, Thailand, Pakistan, the two Yemens, Egypt, Tunisia, Zaire, Gabon and Australia.

Kuwait has been the first non-Muslim oil producer to enter the international field of exploration and production. It enjoys an advantage when competing for concessions in being part of the Third World and in its history as pioneer of generous aid spending to other Third World countries. After the first decade of its operations Kufpec had accumulated heavy losses but this was expected in the early stage of KPC's career as an international oil company. Kuwait has the necessary finance, experience and expertise but a degree of luck is also required. The prospects for the 1990s are that production in several overseas operations such as those in the USA, North Sea, Egypt and Australia will expand rapidly from small beginnings. Kuwait is not going to abandon its role in world-wide oil exploration.

KPC has expanded even more vigorously downstream towards the market. Kuwait now has the third largest refining capacity in OPEC after Saudi Arabia and Venezuela and this is being increased by a further 30 per cent under the current expansion programme. In 1980 its exports of refined products were only one-fifth of crude oil exports; today they are about equal. More and more of these refined products are directed towards

Kuwait's growing retail network in Western Europe. Beginning with the purchase of a small batch of petrol stations in Belgium in 1985, KPC has spread into Italy, Sweden, Denmark, Belgium, the Netherlands and Luxembourg.

A deal to buy Gulf Oil's retail network in the UK fell through because Gulf wanted KPC to buy its Milford Haven refinery. KPC already owned large refineries in the Netherlands and Denmark and was expanding its capacity at home. However, in October 1986 the Kuwait government's investment office bought 830 petrol stations in the UK from Hays Petroleum Services. Throughout Western Europe the new brand-name for Kuwaiti products, Q8 (pronounced 'Kuwait'), began to appear in the autumn of 1986. Showing adaptability and enterprise, KPC also unveiled a new diesel fuel for the Italian market, where a high proportion of privately owned cars run on diesel. The new fuel lacks the normal diesel smell. In March 1987 KPC also bought Ultramor Golden Eagle, which owns or operates 465 service stations in the UK, and doubled its market share in the country to 2 per cent. The corporation's ultimate target is to acquire 7 per cent of the UK market. In 1989 KPC also began to spread into Asia though an agreement with Thailand to set up 200 petrol stations carrying the Q8 logo. Kuwait has come a long way in the fifty years since Shaikh Ahmad Jaber granted the oil concession to the all-powerful British and American companies.

Kuwait is therefore far from being an oil state in the old sense of the term – that is, a country which acts merely as passive host to immensely powerful international companies exploiting its major natural resource in return for a fee. It is itself an active partner in the international oil industry.

However, it remains true that possession of oil is the principal source of Kuwait's wealth and therefore of the exceptional status it enjoys in spite of being one of the smallest countries in the world. So, what measures have the Kuwaitis – both government and people – taken to safeguard their future?

Paul Stevens, a young British economist at the University of Surrey, has put forward the startling view that the verdict from history will be that oil was to the Arabs in the twentieth century what the Mongols were to the Arab world in the thirteenth century – 'an unmitigated disaster'.* The various reasons he gives to support his thesis all relate to the fact that an

*See 'The Impact of Oil on the Role of the State in Economic Development: A Case Study of the Arab World' by Paul Stevens in *Arab Affairs*, quarterly journal of the League of Arab States, No. 1, Summer 1986.

overwhelmingly large oil and gas sector in the economy tends to destroy the basis for what he calls DPAs – directly productive activities. Thus it causes an overvaluation of the exchange rate, which encourages imports and destroys local industries. It distorts the labour market, causes the neglect of agriculture and an 'unreal' expansion in public services. Above all it destroys the incentive to engage in DPAs.

Kuwaitis, both inside and outside the government, have themselves been grappling with these problems. One of Kuwait's leading intellectuals, Muhammad Rumaihi, editor of the weekly magazine *Al-Arabi*, published a book in Arabic in 1983 and in English in 1986 under the title *Beyond Oil: Unity and Development in the Gulf*. In his conclusion he writes:

The Gulf societies are based on a dichotomy between the production of oil on the one hand and the wealth generated by this production on the other. They are held together by a tripartite alliance of the conservative authorities (the ruling clan), the owners of commercial capital, and the top layers of the educated elite. The people of the Gulf are generally divorced from production; they are the recipients of wealth but not its creators.

Rumaihi is not alone in making this kind of comment. Some even sharper opinions on the situation are published in Kuwait, although his book is one of very few to appear in English. The question is whether they are excessively gloomy and critical.

Some of the alarming views of the British economist Paul Stevens about the disastrous consequences of oil wealth do not apply to Kuwait. Kuwait had no agriculture to be neglected, and the attraction of the beduin to the city can hardly be compared with the depopulation of the land by the peasantry in countries such as Algeria or Iraq. The beduin were self-sustaining at a very low standard of living but produced no surplus. However, Stevens's points about the difficulty of stimulating 'directly productive activities' under the shadow of the oil industry and the effect of the 'unreal' expansion in public services are apposite.

From the earliest days of the oil era Kuwaitis became accustomed to a high rate of government spending on public services, which were entirely financed out of oil income rather than taxation. Even today only 15 per cent of government revenues are described as 'non-oil', and most of this is net income from government enterprises. About 5 per cent of total revenues are customs duties; there is no income tax. Health and education services and social security have always been free; housing, water and electricity supplies are heavily subsidized; and salaries paid by the state, which employs about a third of the population, are high. Furthermore, in order to stimulate the economy whenever it showed signs of recession, the government has pursued a policy of buying land at highly inflated prices in order to channel funds into private hands.

Even before the onset of the oil recession made a policy of retrenchment unavoidable it was clear that government expenditure was getting out of hand. In 1982, Abdul Latif al-Hamad, the former director of the Kuwait fund who was then finance minister, warned that the government faced bankruptcy in four years if the increase in government spending was not checked. The crash of the unofficial stock exchange – the Suq al-Manakh – in 1982 and the onset of the oil recession prompted the government for the first time to adopt a comprehensive economic strategy in the form of a five-year plan for 1985–90 which aims to rationalize public expenditure by concentrating on productive expenditure and only the most essential public services. A new atmosphere of austerity prevailed. To an outsider this might not be so apparent, in view of the recent completion of a colossal and splendid new conference centre to accommodate the delegations from forty-four countries, including twenty-three heads of state, who attended the fifth summit conference of the Islamic Conference Organization in Kuwait in January 1987. But, having undertaken to host the conference there was no question of Kuwait abandoning the project. It was essential to show strong nerves in its position near the front line of the Gulf war and it was a question of national pride and honour.

In general, however, there is no mistaking the feeling that the era of easy affluence and the bottomless government purse are over. Many Kuwaitis will tell you that this is something that had to happen and that the previous situation was unhealthy and harmful. This opinion is shared even by some who lost millions in the unofficial stock market crash.

The question is whether the era of easy affluence has irremediably damaged the development of both the mentality and the skills which lead to directly productive activities. It is the entrepreneurial spirit and the financial and business techniques of the twentieth and twenty-first centuries which are required. How have the Kuwaitis responded?

The response, as might be expected, has been mixed. There is a discernible gap between the generations. The older generations, who began their lives in poverty or in an affluence which was only relative to the surrounding austerity, have generally conservative economic attitudes but a hardened spirit of entrepreneurship of the mercantile variety. The younger generations, widely travelled and often partly educated abroad, are entirely at home in the modern world of international business and banking but it is they who have suffered most from the weakening of the links between effort and reward. The overstaffing of the civil service, high government salaries and the distribution of unearned wealth through the land-purchase programme have combined to reduce the incentives for hard work and risk-taking.

But these are gross generalizations. Exceptions are so numerous as to cast doubt upon their validity.

On my first visit to Kuwait in 1958 I was assured that no Kuwaiti businessman would have considered investing in something he could not see, such as a shop or cinema or, more usually, an apartment building. Three years later, at the time of independence, this had already changed and there was a rush to take up the shares in any company that was formed. Kuwaiti contractors were the first to take advantage of the oil boom. On a visit in 1980, I found that eighty Kuwaiti contractors were members of the Kuwaiti Contractors' Union, competing fiercely for a large range of construction projects. A few years later they were the first to be hit by the recession, but in general they have survived without government protection.

The state, on the other hand, clearly had to help manufacturing. In 1961 the government was beginning to encourage the establishment of a variety of new industries by setting up joint enterprises – that is, enterprises run by the state in partnership with private capital. These were concentrated in sectors that were thought either to be too large for private capital alone or socially desirable, such as fisheries, flour mills or transport. The National Industries Company, 51 per cent state-owned, had a variety of plants producing building materials, batteries, detergents, etc. The investors still did not think they were taking serious risks, because the government would always rescue any company in difficulties; nevertheless, the change in attitude had been astonishingly speedy.

Similar qualifications have to be made to the suggestion that the younger generation of Kuwaitis are disinclined to hard work. From my own observation there are at least as many who are prepared to work hard and late as are easy-going to the point of idleness. What is undeniable is that not enough have acquired the type of education or technical skills that the country needs, and, even among those who have, returning to Kuwait with degrees or doctorates in science or engineering, there are many who turn to the less intellectually demanding posts in administration. This is not to deny that those in the higher civil service posts are often extremely industrious. The middle and lower ranks are overmanned; the higher ranks are usually overworked.

Attitudes are continually changing. In the 1980s the government was trying to divert young Kuwaitis of both sexes from the arts departments of the university into the underused technical colleges, but there were signs that the public, aware of the country's requirements, was already responding.

The efforts which began in the 1960s to develop manufacturing industries in order to reduce reliance on oil produced some striking results. Value added in the manufacturing sector increased by an average of over 16 per cent a year between 1974 and 1980 until it was contributing nearly 10 per cent of the non-oil GDP. However, industries were hit by the effects of the oil recession. The sector grew much more slowly, falling to 7.5 per cent of non-oil GDP. In 1984 Kuwait Sanitary Industries suffered a spectacular bankruptcy, and in 1986 the government devised a scheme to buy out a total of thirty-three companies with the express purpose of closing them down. Several others were in difficulties but there were many more, which in some cases had been revamped, that were flourishing. While a continuing government share in the industrial sector was considered necessary, there were many of the new class of private entrepreneurs who believed that it should be reduced to the minimum on the grounds that managers in the public sector were certain to be less efficient and less concerned with profitability.

There are many examples of Kuwaitis who have successfully bridged the gap between the pre-oil era and today. Often the process can be observed within a single family. In one chapter of his outstanding study *The Merchants: The Big Business Families of Arabia* (London, 1984), Michael Field describes a leading Kuwaiti dynasty – the al-Ghanim. Haji Ahmad, the grandfather of Qutayba al-Ghanim, the present head of al-Ghanim Industries, was a dhow owner and sea captain plying the Basra–Bombay route. When he lost his dhow in a disastrous storm in 1925, he and his young son, Yusuf, were obliged to turn to other occupations. Ahmad became a timber merchant, while Yusuf went in for quarrying with considerable success. A visit to Britain just before the Second World War at the Kuwait Oil Company's invitation broadened his horizons. He returned to acquire various importing agencies and in 1947, with support from the ruler, he became sole agent in Kuwait for General Motors. Yusuf was energetic and imaginative. While his competitors were content to deal in gold or speculate in land, he was always ready to try new enterprises. But in other respects he remained conservative, running his business empire as a centralized patriarchy. Finally, in the early 1970s, his son, Qutayba, educated in Scotland and Berkeley, California, persuaded Yusuf to hand over the running of the business to him. Having reorganized and streamlined the empire along advanced modern lines, Qutayba in turn handed over management to his brother and a team of Arabs and Westerners. He was convinced that, in order to maintain growth in the future, his company had to expand into industry. In 1975 he bought Kirby Industries of Houston, Texas, which manufactures pre-engineered steel buildings. When I visited Kuwait in 1980, he had imported an entire Kirby Building Systems plant from Houston, together with 240 American workers, and set it up in the Shuayba industrial zone in Kuwait. The factory has since been Arabized and exports throughout the region. However, by this time, Qutayba had become primarily interested in American investment and was spending much of his time in the United States.

The history of the activities of the al-Ghanim family over the past two generations – from seafaring to commerce to industry – serves as a paradigm for the people of Kuwait. The adaptability and adventurousness that the family has demonstrated give cause for optimism.

On the other hand, it would have required a manic degree of optimism at the beginning of the oil era to look forward to a time when Kuwait could become self-sufficient in agriculture. In the 1950s no one gave the matter much thought. The nation's diet rapidly improved as fresh fruit and vegetables, eggs and meat were imported from Lebanon, Jordan and Iran. But the possibility that the soil and climate of Kuwait could be used to produce enough food to feed the Kuwaitis seemed exceedingly remote.

However, as early as 1952, the government started the first experimental farm at Omariya, near what is now the industrial area of Shuwaykh. Since the shortage of irrigation water was the greatest challenge, trials began on drip irrigation, by which carefully monitored amounts of water and fertilizers are fed to the plant roots and the wastage of the sprinkler system is avoided. This was a novel technique at the time. It was soon realized that a substantial variety of vegetables could be grown in Kuwait – such as tomatoes, marrows, aubergines, peppers and cucumbers – although they had to be protected by some form of greenhouse against the searing summer heat and the fierce sandstorms of spring and early summer. The Omariya farm also entered the field of animal husbandry by trying to develop a breed of dairy cattle which could stand the Kuwaiti climate. The biggest problem was fodder. Cattle will eat almost anything and, according to the present director of the animal husbandry unit, they find a combination of newspapers and chicken manure particularly delectable. But they also need roughage, which means hay and alfalfa. The hay has to be imported and is expensive, but most of the alfalfa can be grown in Kuwait, and experiments continue to produce new combinations of the essential roughage and sources of protein.

With government encouragement agriculture expanded in the 1970s and production doubled between 1980 and 1983. There are some 450 private holdings, mainly in the Wafra and Abdaly areas, ranging from less than 100,000 to one million square metres. Until 1983 the development was fairly haphazard in spite of the government's support but, in that year, a public authority for agriculture and fisheries was set up to devise a twenty-year master-plan and combine the efforts of all the various specialized agricultural companies and syndicates. Like all the Arab Gulf states in the Gulf Cooperation Council, Kuwait has become extremely conscious of the strategic importance of self-sufficiency in food supplies. The reduction of dependence on imports is a major element in state policy. There is a close parallel here with the desire of advanced industrial countries to limit their dependence on imported fuel.

Kuwaitis are under no illusion that self-sufficiency will take less than twenty to thirty years to attain, and even then it cannot include such items as beef and cereals. (Fortunately Saudi Arabia among the GCC states is producing a surplus of cereals. For Kuwait cereal production is considered too expensive and unnecessary, although advances in the technique of treating effluent water for the irrigation of corn and barley may create new possibilities in this field.) Self-sufficiency in poultry, vegetables and fruit is a visible goal; already Kuwait produces 60 per cent of the eggs it needs, 40 per cent of the poultry meat and 100 per cent of the tomatoes. The next emphasis is likely to be on dairy farming and animal husbandry to increase the 25 per cent of the required milk supplies that is produced in the country. The Kuwaitis are very conscious of the fact that urban growth and the hunting of the animals which used to live in the desert, such as rabbits, wolves and gazelles, as well as scores of species of migrating birds which used to stop off in Kuwait, has meant the virtual extinction of wildlife. Animal husbandry can to some extent be seen as compensation. Friesian cows have been brought in from Holland and Denmark, millions of chickens from the Lebanon, Europe and India, and sheep from Turkey, Europe and Australia. The sheep herds are increasing steadily and should reach half a million head when a new sheep farm project is completed near Salabiya. In 1986 fifteen goats were imported by the Omariya farm from Cyprus for breeding purposes, although care will be needed to ensure that this does not conflict with another objective –*tashjeer*, or the 'greening' of Kuwait through the mass planting of shrubs and trees. *Tashjeer* has already progressed a long way as a result both of the planting of private gardens which have now grown to maturity and an ambitious programme of city landscaping. This is to be greatly expanded to include some twenty-three neighbourhood gardens as well as several larger parks and a green belt around the central urban area. Tamarisks, which are sand- and salt-resistant, and over a million palm trees had been planted by 1990.

In view of Kuwait's extremely unpromising natural environment, the key to all its hopes for self-sufficiency lies in research and experiment. Not only the Omariya farm but the country's two main research institutions – the Kuwait Institute for Scientific Research (KISR) and the Kuwait Fund for the Advancement of Sciences (KFAS)* – are engaged in a variety of projects concerned with the hybridization of plants, animal breeding, the increase of yields in desert conditions, the treatment of brackish and effluent water, irrigation methods, and so on. For example, the use of plastic mulching films as a cover for the soil is already widely known as a method of preventing evaporation, reducing soil erosion and retarding weed growth; KISR Petroleum's petrochemical and materials division has taken the process a further stage by developing a nutritional and degradable mulch film which has the same advantages as the regular mulch film, which degrades when the season is over and provides nutrients for the plants, but has no toxic chemical additives. As I saw on a recent visit to the KISR experimental station at Salabiya, this produces remarkable yields of beans, corn and cucumbers. The process has been patented in the USA. A KFAS project concerns 'solar ponds', which consist of three layers of which the lowest is extremely salty, the central is brackish and the top layer is fresh water. Some of the sun's rays penetrate the lowest layer, and are trapped there by the temperatures of up to 92 °C, which leads to the water's gradual desalination. The method has recently come into use in the USA and Australia but Kuwait provides ideal conditions; it should produce fresh water for irrigation at half the present cost.

If agriculture is an industry of the future, fishing, together with pearling, has been a major occupation in Kuwait since the foundation of the state. The first Kuwaitis did not take readily to ocean fishing and it was mostly left to the men of the Awazim tribe, who occupied the coastal villages. Even today with the increase in population and the rise in living standards the local industry provides about 99 per cent of consumption, which is over 5000 tons a year. Kuwaitis still eat more meat than fish but meat is expensive because of the high cost of imported fodder, and fish consumption is growing faster. The *hamour* is usually on the menu, with the delicious *sobaiti* as more of a speciality. But it is the harvesting and eating of shrimps which has progressed most rapidly – doubling in two years during the early

*See Chapter 8.

1980s. The individual fishermen, who still supply two-thirds of the local market, use much of the traditional equipment: drift nets, conical nets, baskets, and screen barriers known locally as *hadra*. Gradually they are acquiring more modern equipment: light plastic boats with engines to replace the wooden dhows and net wire instead of split bamboo. Apart from the individual fishermen, there is a United Fisheries Company, formed in 1971, on the recommendation of FAO, through the amalgamation of three fishing companies who were mainly engaged in shrimping. The aim was to reduce overfishing by concentrating attention on a wider variety of species over a larger fishing area. There are some 258 species of fish in the waters of the Gulf, of which about 30 per cent are edible. The Kuwait Institute for Scientific Research and the Kuwaiti Institute for Marine Fisheries and Navigation, established in 1971, are engaged in a series of projects for developing new hybrids, conservation and the prevention of oil and industrial pollution. Overfishing is a constant problem. A decline in the shrimp catch in the mid-1980s required severe restrictions on the fishing season. But the important fact is that Kuwait's fisheries are now regarded by the government as a major natural resource of great potential. They are seen as one of the most promising means of reducing the country's dependence on oil.

In 1990 the Kuwait government changed its view about prospects for petrochemicals, as it became convinced that after a period of fluctuation and uncertainty the market was due to enter an era of expansion into the next century, based on the steadily growing demands of Third World countries. Plans that had been shelved more than once were revived for a $2 billion petrochemicals complex to be built in the Shuayba industrial zone. Kuwait has some notable comparative advantages in the field. The raw materials of gas and naphtha will be supplied from the expanded and upgraded refineries. The country's shareholdings in international chemical companies will help to ensure outlets. The venture is not without risk because Kuwait faces competition from the petrochemicals of other GCC states, notably Saudi Arabia, and from the protectionism of the European Community over which the GCC states are attempting to negotiate. But the huge investment is another indication that Kuwait does not intend to rely in the future on its exports of crude oil and its income from overseas assets.

Kuwait can try to prolong the life of the country's oil and gas reserves and make as much use of them as possible. It can also attempt to develop alternative industries, although these will always suffer from the very limited size of the internal market and the need to import most of the labour. However, there are other courses available and one of them is to invest the

country's surplus revenues in such a way as to provide an assured income
when the oil begins to decline. This was the motive behind the establishment in 1976 of the reserve fund for future generations, which receives 10
per cent of all state revenues and cannot be touched for twenty-five years.
This is in addition to all the other investments that have been made by the
government both before and since.

The income from the country's total reserves, which in 1990 are
estimated at about $85 billion, is now a major factor in the economy. It
cushioned Kuwait against the effects of the recession of the 1980s. But the
country's rulers and the general public know that investment revenue can
only supplement and not replace the income from other activities. No
Kuwaiti can contemplate a future for his or her country as a rentier state.

From the earliest days Kuwaitis were concerned about how to make the
best use of their resources. Initially the surpluses were very small and were
transferred annually to a reserve account held in London. The Kuwaiti
currency was tied to sterling, which was still a reserve currency, and most
Kuwaiti trade was still directed towards Britain. (The only bank allowed to
operate in Kuwait was the British Bank of the Middle East and oil company
payments were made directly to its headquarters in London.) Kuwait's
investments were divided between British bonds and equities. In 1952 a
Kuwait Investment Board, consisting of five British bankers, was set up in
London and began gingerly diversifying a proportion of Kuwait's reserves
into Europe and the United States. In 1952 the National Bank of Kuwait, the
country's first commercial bank, was established, to be followed in 1960 by
the Gulf Bank and Al-Ahli Bank.

On my first visit to Kuwait in 1958 it was still hard to find Kuwaitis who
did not see their economy as part of the sterling system. (It was also a
common belief that a Kuwaiti loan was keeping the London County Council
going.) It has to be said that the British government and British officials in
the region also looked upon Kuwait's oil wealth as essential to maintain
sterling as an international currency.

The situation began to change rapidly after independence. Kuwait
started to make use of its reserves for direct investment in new enterprises
both at home and abroad. These might be public companies or, more often,
joint enterprises between the state and the private sector. In this way the
Kuwait National Petroleum Company, the Kuwait Flour Mills Company
and the Kuwait Transport Company were all set up in 1962. A series of
investment and financial companies, such as the Kuwait Investment
Company and the Kuwait Hotels Company, were established for both home
and overseas investment and soon acquired an international reputation.

For the management of the country's foreign portfolio the Kuwait Investment Board became the Kuwait Investment Office, managed by Kuwaitis. The investments quickly spread widely in the British, European and American markets. But at the same time Kuwait was developing its role as a source of funds to other Arab countries and many central banks in the Arab states began to receive deposits from Kuwait.

In 1967 the devaluation of sterling by 16 per cent meant the devaluation of the major part of Kuwait's foreign assets. The Kuwait government was obliged to reconsider its entire financial relationship with Britain, although this would sooner or later have been inevitable as sterling was ceasing to be a reserve currency.

When the enormous increase in oil prices and revenues took place in the early 1970s, coinciding with a period of severe dislocation in international financial markets, the management of Kuwait's foreign reserves required difficult decisions of first national importance. As the prices began to rise, reserves were about $1.8 billion, which had been accumulated over the previous twenty years. With the enormous surpluses on current account in the balance of payments which now accrued the reserves shot up at an astronomical rate. Within a decade they had reached $80 billion and were bringing in an income of about $4 billion – equivalent to about half the oil revenues.

The investment policy of the Kuwait government during the 1980s was like that of any prudent individual, combining the aims of safety, income and capital appreciation. The Kuwait Investment Office continued to operate in London but investments in the United States, which became the main area of operations, were handled by agents. Some 60 per cent of the general reserves were in equities, industry and real estate, and 40 per cent in bonds and first-class medium- and long-term securities. In the United States investments were spread among the 'seventy-five companies' on Wall Street – that is, the seventy-five companies regarded as most reliable. But the 1970s also saw a policy of diversifying into other countries, with the purchase of portfolios in Germany, Switzerland, France, Belgium, Holland and Japan, and also into much more speculative enterprises.

Through the Kuwait Investment Company, Kuwait made a widely publicized entrance into the real-estate market. KIC bought Kiawah Island off the Atlantic coast of the United States to turn it into a holiday resort. In London it shrewdly bought St Martin's Properties with its wide network of interests at a time when the property market was temporarily depressed.

Kuwait soon became a leading participant in international financial operations. Its policy was to shun publicity by seeking control through property or insurance companies rather than acting directly. But anonymity is not always possible – especially in countries which require disclosure. Kuwait became a prime target in a hostile campaign against the 'oil shaikhs', who were, with ludicrous exaggeration, accused of buying up the British heritage or the key landmarks of the American economy. In time the West has become accustomed to the idea of Kuwait as an important international investor, and the country's activities no longer arouse resentment or alarm. By the end of the 1970s it owned a substantial slice of the Champs Elysées, a share in the German Daimler Benz company, another in British Lonrho, a hotel complex in Atlanta, Georgia, and other pieces of property from Latin America to the Far East. In a typical operation in October 1986 the Kuwait Investment Office acquired a 5 per cent stake in Spain's biggest commercial bank, Banco Central, in a deal completed through a Swiss firm. Previously the KIO had bought a large stake in the Spanish paper-making industry. In the same month Kuwait increased its already substantial holdings in Singaporean real estate, light industrial and brokerage firms with a $4 million investment in United Overseas Land, a property development firm.

With the downturn in the oil market and the subsequent recession in the mid-1980s, Kuwait's reserves were crucial. In spite of big cuts in expenditure, the country's investment income had to be used to cover the budget deficit. In 1986–87, the deficit exceeded the investment income and for the first time a drawing-down of reserves had to be contemplated. There was a problem: more than half the reserves are in the Reserve Fund for Future Generations (RFFG) which cannot be touched until 2001, while much of the remainder – the State General Reserve – is illiquid because it is in the form of long-term loans to Arab countries or tied up in local investments. The choice was between further cuts in spending or a resort to borrowing. Although this meant that the government had little room to manoeuvre – a position to which it was quite unaccustomed – it was hard to look on the situation as cause for serious alarm. With state reserves of $80 billion, even if slightly depleted, reserves in private hands of about the same quantity, a population of fewer than 2 million and with the country's modern infrastructure largely completed, Kuwait needs only a modest degree of financial prudence to see it through the lean times. This remains true even if the price of oil remains at $15–18 per barrel for some time before rising again in the mid-1990s as the Kuwaitis expect.

Spain has been the country in which Kuwait's investments have had their biggest impact. In the 1980s these amounted to some $2 billion, making Kuwait Spain's biggest foreign investor. Apart from paper-making

Kuwait came to own 70 per cent of Spain's fertilizer industry and its largest food-processing group. The operations were all conducted from the Kuwait Investment Office in London through the KIO's Spanish representative, the flamboyant Catalan financier Javier de la Rosa. In contrast to the normal extreme discretion of KIO's operations, those in Spain have been the subject of constant attention and comment in the Spanish press.

In 1988, however, KIO's low profile in London could not be maintained. When the Thatcher government decided to proceed with the privatization of its shares in British Petroleum in spite of the stock market crash of October 1987, KIO bought 22 per cent of what is Britain's largest company. Alarmed at the consequences of an OPEC member acquiring such a large stake in the British oil industry, the British government, backed by some concern expressed in parliament and the press, obliged Kuwait to reduce its holding to below 10 per cent. Although Kuwait made a substantial profit from the operation, the Kuwait government was both hurt and angry, feeling that its purchase had helped to save the British government from a major embarrassment and that although Kuwait was patently a friendly country to Britain it had suffered what amounted to racial discrimination.

Partly as a consequence of this affair, Kuwait began to reduce its holdings in the London stock market. But it also had reason to feel that the New York and Tokyo stock markets were overvalued. The trend was distinctly towards increasing investment in Western Europe. It was wholly character-istic that in 1990 Kuwait should be the first of the Arab Gulf states to sound out the prospects for investment in the countries of Eastern Europe as they began to switch from command to market economies.

Kuwait has indisputably become an international investor of promi-nence. But this is not the same as saying that the country has become a major financial centre. On a visit just before independence, I wondered whether Sharia Fahd al-Salem, the first street in Kuwait with modern buildings, was destined to become the Wall Street of the Arab world. This is not precisely what has happened. Some twenty years later I recorded my impression that Kuwaitis were still 'hovering on the brink of the shark-infested sea of international finance'. They still had not made up their minds whether they wanted the Kuwaiti dinar to become an international currency or whether their economy was big enough to sustain it. The Kuwait stock exchange, although it had one of the highest turnovers in the world, was still limited to the shares of Kuwaiti companies. With its modest rows of plastic-covered benches, it gave the impression of a social club for businessmen rather than a professional market.

A financial centre requires both the demand for and the supply of financial facilities. Kuwait had the necessary infrastructure of telecommunications and air transport but, although domestic demand for finance was increasing during the 1970s, it was still very small in relation to the supply of funds because of the lack of opportunities for domestic investment. Consequently the commercial banks held huge foreign assets and substantial deposits in Kuwaiti currency with the central bank.

With the enormous flow of funds seeking outlets in the narrowly restricted Kuwaiti market, sharp fluctuations in the Kuwait stock exchange were inevitable. Share prices rose by 134.7 per cent in 1976 but collapsed in 1977. The Kuwait government then suspended the formation of public companies in order to enable the market to absorb those companies which had been newly created. It also restricted to a minimum the increase in capital of existing companies. The ban was partially lifted in 1979, but by then Kuwaiti investors had begun forming companies in other Gulf states, such as Bahrain and the UAE, where there were few or no restrictions.

Because the shares of these public Gulf companies could not be traded on the Kuwait stock exchange, an unofficial and semi-illegal exchange developed. First it was sited in the old Jat ('clover') market, scattered in small brokers' booths among the little shops selling clothes and perfumes. As business expanded this became impossibly inconvenient and in 1978 it was moved to a modest two-storey rented building in the Suq al-Manakh at the centre of the city's commercial life. (*Manakh*, like most Arabic words, has more than one meaning. It is 'climate' and the 'place where you tether your camel'.)

In this way the extraordinary four-year phenomenon of the Suq al-Manakh began. Trading was even more fevered than on the official stock exchange. A boom in 1978 was followed by two years of recession but then, in 1981, in the wake of the new round of oil-price rises set off by the outbreak of the Iraq–Iran war, there was an explosion of trading activity. Some 3.5 billion Gulf shares were exchanged, with a market value of $6 billion. Prices fluctuated virtually at the will of the company owners. Every Kuwaiti seemed to have caught the Manakh fever. The modest Suq al-Manakh building acted as a huge gambling casino which had the nation enthralled.

The wild speculative boom was bound to end with a crash like the Wall Street crisis of 1929. It was only a question of when. Gloom over the prospects of a prolonged Gulf war was a factor, but the immediate cause, in August 1982, was the failure of one of the biggest speculators to honour a postdated cheque he had written for 55 million Kuwaiti dinars ($180 million). The bubble burst, leaving a trail of entangled debt totalling more than $90 billion from 29,000 postdated and unhonoured cheques.

It was a sharp shock to the national psyche. Probably only about 6000 individuals were directly affected, but in Kuwait's tightly knit society everyone has at least a close relative or friend who was involved. My own experience is that, while some Kuwaitis are willing and even eager to tell you how much they lost, others are extremely reticent. Among the big losers the experience of one extremely prominent businessman who is also a lawyer is no doubt typical. He said that, while he owed 12 million dinars, as a result of the crash he was owed 14 million dinars. The trouble was that all his debtors were bankrupt.

The government mounted a rescue operation. It spent 756 million dinars from the State General Reserve to maintain share prices and a further 500 million dinars to reimburse small investors. Only eighty-eight individuals were declared bankrupt, but in a further rescue operation in 1986 the government bought up thirty-three 'closed' companies for a total of 227 million dinars.

With hindsight the government knew that it had been a grave mistake to have provoked the creation of an unofficial stock exchange through its own restrictive legislation and then failed to legalize it and bring it under control. Fresh legislation governing the official stock exchange, housed in a magnificent new building, is designed to ensure that such a speculative boom and crash are not repeated.

Five years after the crash its consequences were still being felt, as the government's rescue package proved extremely difficult to complete. The biggest debtors were standing out for even more generous terms in the rescheduling of their debts – especially when the closure of the National Assembly in July 1986 removed a body which was closely scrutinizing the government's actions for fear of excessive generosity. It seemed that the final bill to close the account would be heavy.

What will be the long-term effect on Kuwait's reputation as an international financial centre? The damage seems likely to be limited, if only because Kuwait had not progressed very far in that direction when the crash occurred. The biggest casualty was the Kuwaiti dinar bond market, which had been regarded as a forerunner for Kuwait's aspiring inter-national capital market. Interest in bonds collapsed when shares reached exaggerated prices in 1981–82 and has not recovered since the crash. But in general the Suq al-Manakh was an internal affair which did not reflect the true state of the Kuwaiti economy.

Meanwhile some vital lessons had been learned by both the government and individual investors, and they will not be easily forgotten. The powers of the Kuwait central bank were increased to an extent that it had more authority than any other central monetary authority in the Gulf region. In a lecture to the Kuwait Economic Society in February 1987, the governor of the central bank, Shaikh Salem Abdul Aziz al-Sabah, outlined his ideas for Kuwait's future as a financial centre through the use of these powers to trade in shares and bonds, the further extension of the central bank's supervisory role combined with a more flexibly managed monetary policy and improved coordination between monetary and fiscal policy.

After thirty years with very large funds to invest, Kuwaitis and their government have built up a substantial body of expertise. The ultimate prospects for Kuwait as a financial centre are good, provided this expertise is enhanced by failure as well as success.

8

Bodies and Minds

In 1932, 4000 Kuwaitis – about 4 per cent of the population – died in a smallpox epidemic. By 1949 the situation regarding health care had altered very little. There were only four doctors in the country. One of them, the first Arab doctor to come from Palestine, remembers working at that time in the country's sole primitive hospital, where there was electric power for only two hours a day and he had to give orders for all instruments to be boiled for at least ten minutes.

Rapid change began in 1950, when the influx of the first substantial oil revenues coincided with the accession of Shaikh Abdallah al-Salem, who decided that the country should have modern medical services as soon as possible and that they should be free for everyone, including non-Kuwaiti immigrants. By 1967 there were 400 doctors in the government health system and in 1986 there were 2692 (including 250 in the private sector) – a ratio of 1 to 608 of the population. There were 5886 hospital beds, or 1 to 288 in the population. More than 6 per cent of total budget expenditure in Kuwait is devoted to health. The country is divided into six health areas, each with its own public hospital, health centre, general and specialized clinics, but because of the small size of Kuwait much of the specialized treatment is provided centrally at al-Sabah hospital – the first original public hospital, which stands on the south-western outskirts of Kuwait City.

Al-Sabah has grown into one of the largest health complexes in the world, comprising eight specialized hospitals and centres for chest diseases, cancer, psychiatry, allergies, orthopaedics, maternity services and kidney transplants.

Within the complex there is an Islamic medical centre. This originated at a highly successful conference on Islamic medicine held in Kuwait in 1981. In 1984 the Amir issued a decree creating an Islamic organization for Medical Sciences. Although it is funded by the government, like many similar Kuwaiti institutions, the organization enjoys a large measure of independence. Funds for the magnificent new copper-domed building which has housed it since the end of 1986 were donated by a private individual. The centre might be said to offer alternative medicine but this would be misleading. Certainly the organization's research department studies traditional herbal medicines of the kind that were prescribed by the great Muslim doctor Ibn Sina, or Avicenna (980–1037), whose treatise *Qanun fil-Tibb* (*The Canon of Medicine*) was used in Europe until the eighteenth century. The researchers try to explain how they work according to modern pharmacological theory. Traditional herbal remedies from the classical period are used at the centre to treat such ailments as diabetes, rheumatism and bronchial asthma. But underlying their work is a belief that the Islamic religion has a unique contribution to make to the art of healing which is not an alternative but complementary to modern medicine. The Amiri decree founding the organization stated its aim as: 'To revive the doctrines of the Islamic religion relating to the treatment and protection against various physical and psychological ailments.' The organization therefore enters into the field of Islamic jurisprudence – and endeavours to evolve an Islamic response to some of the moral questions raised by advances in medical science. Two international seminars – one on 'Reproduction in the Light of Islam' held in 1984, and another on 'Life and Death' in 1985 – brought together medical experts and jurists from all over the Islamic world. These delegates reached the conclusion that, for example, test-tube babies are acceptable to Islam provided that certain rules are adhered to. The sperm and ovum must come from a husband and wife and the procedure must be carried out during the marriage period when both partners are alive. The second seminar discussed the problems presented by life-support machines and the actual moment of death after which the removal of organs for transplant operations was permissible.

There is no equivalent of the papacy in Islam to pronounce on these vital twentieth-century problems, which can only be considered through discussion between Muslim scientists and jurists in this manner. The little state of Kuwait has used its resources to play an advanced role in this area, which is of service to the whole Islamic world.

In 1982 life expectancy in Kuwait was sixty-nine years for men and seventy-four years for women and is increasing steadily. Infant mortality fell from 44.3 per thousand in 1974 to 19 per thousand in 1983. These figures are now comparable with those in the advanced industrial countries. They are not entirely attributed to the vastly improved medical services, which in forty years have changed from slightly above zero to being among the best in the world. The clean water supply, a better diet and immensely improved housing have all made their contributions. Subsidies have helped those with lower incomes, and a comprehensive social security system provides for old age, death, disability and accidents for all Kuwaiti citizens. Pensions, which are a minimum 65 per cent of basic salaries, are paid to widows and the disabled, and to citizens who have reached the age of fifty or who have been in employment for twenty years even if they are below fifty. There is no fixed age for retirement – a fact which has recently come in for some criticism. At a seminar held by the Kuwaiti League of Social Scientists in Februrary 1987 an eminent lawyer pointed out that 69 per cent of Kuwaitis in their fifties had already retired and so deprived the country of a valuable part of its workforce. The pension fund is self-sufficient with contributions from employers, employees and a small state subsidy. At the institution for social security, which was founded in 1977, there are rows of bright and efficient young Kuwaiti girls with direct access to computerized files on each Kuwaiti family who are ready to inform anyone of his or her entitlements. In 1977 a Kuwaiti club for the disabled was founded – the first of its kind in the Arab world. The country has taken a lead in encouraging sport for the disabled in the Gulf region and in recent years has spread its contacts further afield. In October 1986 the Kuwaiti newspapers were full of the achievements of Nizar Ramadan, a young Kuwaiti bound to a wheelchair, who beat the world record for 10,000 metres by five minutes at the Stoke Mandeville games in Britain. In addition, Kuwait has a society for the handicapped and an association for the blind, which cooperate closely.

It is hardly surprising that Kuwaitis, having virtually eliminated the ailments of the developing world, have begun to suffer from those of the advanced industrial countries, such as heart disease and certain forms of cancer. When I visited Kuwait in the early 1960s, I observed at a kindergarten the physical difference between the chubby, doe-eyed children and the lean fathers who arrived to pick them up. The parents had grown up in the years of poverty. A glance at many Kuwaiti family groups today shows that obesity has become a serious problem – especially among the young. Kuwaiti national dress carries its own danger. It is possible to gain 20 pounds under your *dishdasha* before having to alter it or buy a new one. No such evasion is possible with trousers. Kuwaiti parents are becoming conscious of the problems. Sports facilities are lavish but, if the young do not engage in them, or give them up for a sedentary life, the results are obvious and sometimes catastrophic. Articles on the need for exercise and a more nutritious diet have begun to appear in the press and a few lonely joggers can be observed. For about two years the ministry of public health has conducted a serious campaign against smoking, which is now much more prevalent than in the advanced industrial countries. But above all the ministry of public health is concerned with the effects of industrial expansion and twentieth-century economic development in increasing environmental pollution.

The Kuwaiti climate is quite healthy in spite of the extreme summer heat; the biggest natural hazard is dust. But to this is added the pollution from the half a million vehicles in Kuwait City and the discharge from factories, desalination plants and power stations into the atmosphere and the waters of the Gulf. Kuwait became engaged in anti-pollution as early as 1964, when it passed a law imposing a fine of 40,000 dinars on any oil tanker causing oil pollution in Kuwaiti waters. In 1980 the government established an environmental protection council on which fifteen ministries and organizations were represented to formulate a collective policy. Hardly a week passes without discussion of some aspect of the subject in one of Kuwait's favourite activities – a public *nadwa*, or seminar.

There is good reason to hope that Kuwait will avoid reaching a Los Angeles level of pollution, but it has to be said that the greatest single hazard to the health and lives of Kuwaitis is the automobile. The road accident level is one of the highest in the world and the most common cause of death in young males. (Kuwaiti girls drive but are generally safer.) Kuwaitis freely admit that it is an inevitable consequence of the sudden jump from a poverty-stricken desert culture to an advanced standard of living. 'What can you expect,' they say, 'when an adoring father gives his seventeen-year-old son the keys to a new Mercedes?' An additional hazard is created by bus-drivers from the Indian subcontinent, who arrive with licences of mysterious origin and drive their buses 'like dodgems at a fair'. Somewhat belatedly, the government is now confronting the matter with great seriousness and a series of measures is being introduced including new methods of detecting and fining offenders, and educating the public, beginning with youth in schools, in the highway code.

Young Kuwaitis are now among the most highly educated in the Arab world. Literacy among ten- to fourteen-year-olds is 96 per cent for males and 91 per cent for females. The comparable figures for those over sixty is 28 per cent and 6 per cent. In the population as a whole, 12.6 per cent have a secondary school certificate and 4.1 per cent a university degree, although the proportions are rapidly increasing. The reason for the enormous discrepancy between the generations in the matter of formal education is easy to account for. Until the beginning of this century education was confined to the Quranic schools, or *kuttabs*, which were usually endowed by one of the wealthy merchants. A few individuals who might or might not be one of the *ulema*, or religious scholars, acquired great learning and some of this would be disseminated through the *diwaniyahs*. (*Diwaniyah* originally meant the men's quarters in a beduin tent but has since come to mean an association or fraternity.) These were occasions of discussion and debate at which a book might be read or poetry recited. It was by no means a society without culture, although books were a rarity and there were no newspapers or magazines.

It is said that the impetus behind the establishment of Kuwait's first school other than a *kuttab* came in 1910 at a *diwaniyah* of a leading shaikh, when the outstanding Kuwaiti poet of the time, Sayed Yassin al-Tabtabai, eloquently urged on those present the need for proper schools and teachers because 'we cannot follow the path of the prophet unless we know the story of his life – and this we can only learn by study'. His listeners were so impressed that they set about collecting money, which came mainly from wealthy merchants in Bombay, and with this set up the country's first school in a house donated by the al-Khalid family. It was named Al-Mubarakiya after Mubarak the Great, who was ruler at the time.

This was a beginning, but the Mubarakiya school was very modest in its achievements, as it taught little more than religious studies and the techniques of pearl-diving and commerce. In 1920, with the encouragement of the new Amir, Shaikh Ahmad Jaber, a group of Kuwaitis opened a second school offering a wider range of subjects. The thirst for education was still far from satisfied, as Kuwait was broadening its contacts with the outside world, so in 1936 the Amir agreed to an increase of half a per cent in customs duties in order to set up a council of education of its leading citizens, who then imported four qualified teachers from Palestine to lay the foundations of an educational programme using teachers from the Arab world. Until 1942 young Kuwaitis had to go abroad for their secondary education, but between 1942 and 1952 secondary schools were established, and in 1952 the Egyptian ministry of education was persuaded to recognize the Kuwait secondary school certificate.

The growth of education was steady but extremely slow. By 1949 there were 4600 children in school, still less than 1 per cent of the population. But the first influx of oil revenues in the 1950s marked the beginning of an educational explosion as the Amir, Abdallah Salem, laid down the principle that every Kuwaiti boy and girl should be able to go to school. This was enshrined in the 1961 constitution, which states in Article 40 that 'Education is a right for all Kuwaitis . . .' and 'Education in its preliminary stages shall be compulsory and free in accordance with the Law,'

Two new secondary schools – one for boys and another for girls – were founded in 1953 and 1954, and the policy was established that all secondary school graduates would be sent abroad on scholarships if they wished to finish their higher education. In 1955 two distinguished Egyptian educationalists were brought in to make a study of the state of education in the country and their recommendations formed the basis of the system for many years. The seven years of primary education and five years of secondary education were changed to the present system of four years each of primary, intermediate and secondary education.

Egyptian, Palestinian, Syrian and other Arab teachers were imported in large numbers. The number of pupils grew with extraordinary speed – to 20,000 in 1957 and 120,000 in 1967, or nearly 20 per cent of the total population. Today the number is over half a million, or more than 30 per cent of the population, attending schools or other centres of education. There are 592 state schools, about 90 private schools and 9 major centres of higher education, with a total of nearly 30,000 teachers and instructors at all levels.

From the start of the expansion the authorities encouraged all secondary school students to continue with higher education. They even discriminated positively in favour of girls – setting a limit to the number of scholarships for boys but not for girls. The ministry of education annual report for 1956–57 said:

It is a matter of great pride that all girl students who completed their secondary education in the general science section and about 85 per cent of the girls who completed their secondary education in the general arts section and were willing to continue their education were sent to universities in countries abroad.

If Kuwait was to administer its own affairs and policies the need for a well educated younger generation was apparent. The public responded and it soon became the aspiration of Kuwaiti parents that all their sons and daughters should have not only secondary but higher education, even if only a tiny minority of the fathers (let alone the mothers) had been to university themselves. I recall meeting in 1961 a leading merchant who spoke of his eldest daughter who would shortly return from the University of London with a Ph.D in psychology. His respect for her accomplishment outweighed his nervousness about her reaction to the still deeply conservative social life in Kuwait.

In 1960, a year before independence, the ministry of education approached UNESCO for a feasibility study for Kuwait's own university. It was carried out by a three-man team of eminent British, Egyptian and

Palestinian academics. They approved the principle but insisted that it would require careful and lengthy planning.

The government responded by appointing a director and university council to carry out the planning. But immediately it came up against a surprising degree of opposition from various quarters. The radical nationalist group in the National Assembly accused the government of merely seeking prestige and said it would be better to spend the money on health and social welfare. Other members of the Kuwaiti elite expressed the fear that Kuwait lacked the intellectual and scientific milieu to sustain a university. Supporters of the project replied that a university would be the best means of creating such a milieu. In typical Kuwaiti fashion the debate was vigorous and hard-hitting, but gradually the view gained ground that a university was both necessary and feasible. Additional arguments which carried weight were that some of the young Kuwaitis going abroad were suffering from homesickness and financial stress, and also that it was becoming increasingly difficult to find places for all of them.

The government slightly changed its tactics by announcing in 1965 that it would establish two teacher training colleges – one for men and another for women. It was hard for anyone to deny that Kuwait needed to train its own teachers as well as rely on other Arabs. But when these were opened in 1966 they offered, in addition to their role as advanced teacher training colleges, degrees in art, science and education. The nucleus of Kuwait University had been created.

The university soon expanded. In 1967 a college of law and *sharia* (Islamic law) and another for commerce, economics and political science were opened. There was a demand for subjects of immediately applicable value in a rapidly developing city-state. Colleges of engineering and petroleum, medicine and post-graduate studies followed in the 1970s.

In 1975 the university underwent what is now called its first revolution when it switched from the old Egyptian model of degree courses to the American system of 'credit hours', which was said to be more flexible and suitable for Kuwait's needs. One of the reasons was undoubtedly the numbers of Kuwaitis who had graduated in the United States and were now starting to hold key positions in the university administration.

The two original colleges were single-sex institutions but gradually the university became co-educational. Girls were allowed to enrol in any of the faculties except that of law and *sharia*, and the original university college for women remains. Boys and girls attend the same classes, although they sit separately, and the university cafeterias have adjacent halls for males and females.

The question of co-education at Kuwait University has been extremely sensitive. It was opposed by conservative opinion and in 1971 a majority of the National Assembly voted against its extension to other parts of the educational system. In the university itself militant Muslim students belonging to the Social Reform Society denounced co-education as un-Islamic and in their magazine gave lurid accounts of the kind of immorality they claimed was the consequence. In response the National Union of Kuwaiti Students vigorously defended the practice; editorials in the union's magazine, *Ittihad*, described the emancipation of Kuwaiti girls as essential for the country's progress and described its opponents as obscurantist reactionaries. The dispute culminated in an affray on 13 November 1971, which has become famous in the university's history, when a group of fundamentalist students tried to break up a meeting called by the National Union to discuss the whole question of co-education.

Despite the growth of Islamic feeling among the students during the 1970s, co-education no longer seems to be a burning issue. Possibly one of the reasons is that the girls form a clear majority of the students in all the faculties except that of engineering (where they are about 40 per cent). The main reason for this is that the proportion of Kuwaiti boys who go to universities abroad is much higher than that of girls, but there is also no doubt that Kuwaiti girls in general have as much desire for a university education as the boys. In many ways the girls are more highly motivated and more competitive. They consistently obtain better results in examinations.

Because the girls are a majority on the university campus, they are not the object of special interest, as girl undergraduates were in Western universities until sixty years ago. In fact they tend to dominate the campus. Most of the girls have adopted Islamic dress of the nun-like enveloping head-scarf, or *hijab*, but a large minority wear Western dress – some of them in the latest fashions. My own impression is that the proportion wearing Islamic dress is now stationary or even slightly declining. This may be due to the receding influence of the Iranian Islamic Revolution. One who had abandoned the *hijab* said she has asked herself 'why she should do what Khomeini told her'. Girls in Islamic and Western dress mix freely and the variations seem natural. It is quite wrong to suppose that those in the *hijab* are shy or unduly deferential in their attitude towards men. On the contrary, they are full of a self-confidence which makes clear that it was their decision alone to adopt it. Young Kuwaiti girls in the *hijab* are said to be rather more aggressive behind the wheel of a car than their sisters in Western dress.

The university has added greatly to Kuwait's intellectual and cultural life in the twenty-one years of its existence. Despite its importance to the state it has enjoyed a large measure of freedom from government interference. Its twelve splendid libraries are growing steadily; it has created a major information centre on Kuwait and the Arabian Gulf, with data archives and manuscript and document units. It has been especially active in the field of international cooperation with centres of learning both in the Arab states and the rest of the world. One typical activity has been its joint publication with the Institute of Palestine Studies of the unique *Journal of Palestine Studies*.

This does not mean that there is no questioning of the current and future role of the university. In fact, in 1986–87 there were a number of voices saying that Kuwait needed a 'scientific revolution' in the field of higher education. Some felt that admission to the university was too easy and should be made more competitive, although this was strongly resisted by others, as it has been recently in France and Spain, where students insisted that higher education is the right of every citizen. There were demands that the proportion of non-Kuwaiti Arabs should be reduced but others felt that it was an obligation for Kuwait to provide equal educational opportunities for the children of Arab immigrants and that funds should be spent on this rather than on new campus buildings. There were suggestions that Kuwait should set up special schools and colleges for exceptionally gifted children – an experiment which has been tried in Tunisia – but this was opposed as socially divisive and contrary to Kuwait's traditions.

There was one point on which there was almost universal agreement: the need for fewer arts graduates and more with some form of technical training – or applied education, as it is called in Kuwait. In the 1950s young Kuwaitis showed no taste for technical training at all. A splendid new technical school, opened in 1957, had to be used partly as a primary school and partly to train non-Kuwaitis. Now it is realized that any policy of Kuwaitization means that Kuwaitis have to acquire technical skills. It is estimated that the country will need 34,000 skilled workers in the 1990s but, as one noted Kuwaiti educationalist has said, 'Technical education should be twenty years ahead of the needs of development but ours is twenty years behind, which means that the industrialized countries are forty years ahead of us.'

As an urgent measure, the government set up in 1982 an independent public authority for applied education and training to coordinate the activities of all the thirteen training institutes in Kuwait. These offer academic education as well as technical or vocational training.

Today there are marked signs of a change in public attitude and a rise in the prestige of applied education colleges as compared with the university. In 1986–87, 5000 new students entered the applied education colleges, of whom some 2200 had qualified for entrance to the university. The oil recession and cuts in government spending have been contributory factors as they have made all Kuwaitis realize that a university degree – especially in an arts subject – is no longer a guarantee of employment.

Writing in a collection of essays published in 1983 under the title *Arab Resources: the Transformation of a Society* (ed. Ibrahim Ibrahim, London and Washington), the distinguished Arab American Dr A. Samir Anabtawi, professor of political science at Vanderbilt University, deplored the fact that, although there are some sixty universities in the Arab world, 'the majority of Arab doctoral education continues to take place in Europe, the United States and the Soviet Union' and he added that:

only two out of every five Arab researchers actually work in the Arab world. In terms of scientific activity and technical innovation the level of discovery in the Arab world of the 1980s does not even come close to the gains made in a number of western countries half a century or more ago.

This is a situation with the most serious implications for the future of the Arabs, who have set their heart on acquiring and understanding the technology of the advanced industrial nations. Kuwait's contribution towards combating the trend has been considerable; in relation to its small population, it is enormous. The Kuwait Institute for Scientific Research (KISR) was opened in 1967 and has since received enthusiastic government support. It has an annual budget of more than £40 million and a staff of about 350, who include many Arab Americans and other Westerners of Arab origin. The proportion of Kuwaitis on the staff has been steadily increasing, and in 1986 a thirty-five-year-old Kuwaiti chemical engineer, Dr Hamoud al-Roqbah, took over as director. In the same year, KISR moved into splendid new premises.

KISR concentrates on research in areas of special importance to the country and region. Its food resources programme has covered such things as fish culture and the upgrading of sheep and poultry. It has achieved worldwide recognition for its work in producing simple cell protein (SCP) to be used as fodder. Not surprisingly, it has a petroleum, petrochemical and materials division, which has concentrated on such matters as evaluation of Kuwait's oil reserves, the use of catalysts in oil refining and the combating of corrosion, but recently, as we have seen, this division has made a breakthrough into agriculture with the development of a plastic mulch which has greatly increased yields. Another division relates to the environment – marine pollution, coastal and geological surveys, the problem of moving sands, and improvements in building technology. New technology projects cover solar energy, electronics and laser applications and decision-support systems. KISR now responds to a great variety of requests from government ministries and other institutions for support services. It assisted the ministry of planning in the development of a model for Kuwait's next five-year plan.

For the layman the principles of some KISR projects are simple, while others are mysterious. My own curiosity is most aroused by anything related to water resources, and especially the desalination of sea water. The implications of any breakthrough to a cheap method for taking the salt out of the ocean are too obvious to require emphasis.

The use of small water-distillation plants on ships was common from early in the century but since it only produced an equivalent amount of water from steam it was expensive and could only be conducted on a limited scale. A unit of this kind was brought into Kuwait from a ship in 1950. It was Professor R.S. Silver, whose name should no doubt be better known than it is, who developed the multi-stage flash process which was gradually improved to reduce the amount of energy to produce a gallon of water and therefore the cost. A multi-stage flash distillation plant – the first of its kind in the world – was opened in Kuwait in 1958, producing 300 million gallons per day. The water was so pure that some minerals had to be put back to give the water an acceptable taste.

But it was still an expensive method. The principle of the alternative, known as reverse osmosis, has been known for about two hundred years. In very simple terms it means placing a semi-permeable membrane between sea water and fresh water. The fresh water will diffuse into the sea water through osmosis until the concentration of salt is equal on both sides, but if the process can be reversed by increasing the pressure on the salt-water side to exceed the osmotic pressure a flow of fresh water can be produced. Unlike the multi-stage flash system, no heating is required because there is no change from liquid to vapour but only from liquid to liquid. The plant requires little land. The components are mostly low-cost plastics and there is little corrosion. It is therefore much cheaper. The difficulty has been to find a membrane that will stand the strain and not speedily become spoiled. It works very well for brackish water but not for sea water.

In 1984 KISR began a project in partnership with West Germany to set up a reverse osmosis pilot plant at the East Doha power station on the Kuwaiti coast with the object of testing different types of membrane, reducing deterioration and experimenting in every way to reduce the cost. The plant is producing 850,000 gallons of water per day from the sea but its importance lies in research and development. The West Germans have completed their part of the programme and KISR is carrying on alone.

Not everyone is convinced of the overriding importance of reverse osmosis technology. Some think that the multi-stage flash will continue to be used and improved. Obviously much depends on the price of fuels. If the price of oil falls, reverse osmosis will lose some of its advantage. My own feeling, which is no more scientific than a feeling, is that it could be the basis for a revolution in life in a desert environment.

Apart from KISR, Kuwait has a younger institution which might appear to be a rival but is in fact complementary. This is the Kuwait Foundation for the Advancement of Science (KFAS), which was established in 1976 on the personal initiative of the Amir, Shaikh Jaber al-Ahmad, who continues regularly to chair the meetings of its board of directors. The Amir discussed the idea with Abdul Aziz al-Saqr, the chairman of the Kuwait Chamber of Commerce, and it was agreed that Kuwaiti shareholding companies would contribute 5 per cent of their annual net profits to KFAS; these are supplemented by large private donations from individuals and local companies. It constitutes an outstanding example of collaboration between the ruling family and the merchants. The fund might be compared to the Ford Foundation or the Carnegie Trust but it was the first of its kind in the Arab world. (Others have since followed, such as the huge King Faisal Foundation in Saudi Arabia.)

Dr Ali al-Shemlan, the young Kuwaiti director-general of KFAS, explains that KFAS does not restrict itself to Kuwait but tries to promote scientific progress in other Arab and Islamic states. It funds research and training scholarships as well as providing for prizes and awards to students, authors, translators and researchers. It supports both basic and applied research, with the latter concentrating especially on energy and food resources. It makes research grants for unsolicited proposals initiated by scientists which have in the past been in such fields as marine biology and geo-study, both in Kuwait and the Arabian Gulf, mathematics, microbiology and chemistry. In many projects it works jointly with KISR but unlike KISR it does no research of its own but sponsors others. These people may be in KISR or Kuwait University but also abroad, where the only condition is that the work should be sponsored by Kuwaiti national organizations, such as a current project at the Trieste International Centre for Physics. In such cases the projects are sent for approval by expert opinion abroad.

Dr al-Shemlan talks with enthusiasm about the publishing programme for original works and translations which started in 1981 and has already produced sixty titles. He is very conscious of the fact that the Golden Age of Islam, centred on Abbasid Baghdad in the eighth century, began with the systematic translation of all the outstanding works of the classical period in Greek, Latin and Sanskrit before the Arab/Islamic empire produced great original works of its own. To the same purpose KFAS invites foreign scientists and scholars to symposia and funds Kuwaiti PhDs to go abroad to read papers or attend refresher courses.

In addition to publishing, KFAS awards a variety of prizes for authorship, translation and publishing. These are made at the annual Arabic book fair held in conjunction with the National Council for Arts and Letters. The most prestigious are the two Kuwait prizes – one for Kuwaitis and another for citizens of other Arab states – which are awarded in each of the five fields of basic science, applied science, arts and letters, Arabic and Islamic culture, and economic and social sciences, with ten prizes of 20,000 dinars (about £48,000) being awarded each year. In 1985 the first prize was awarded to a woman, an Egyptian scientist Dr Venice Gouda, for her work in the field of corrosion. Other prizes include an Islamic medicine prize, which is presented in recognition of work in physical and psychological health according to Islamic law, and the agricultural prize, which is presented six times a year to members of the local farmers' union.

Both the Amir and the director-general undoubtedly see one of the main purposes of KFAS as awakening and broadening interest in the sciences among the Kuwaiti public. The fund organizes popular science programmes for television. I watched an excellent one on Halley's Comet. It also arranges camping holidays for young Kuwaitis in the desert or on the shores of the Gulf to make them more aware of their natural environment and encourage them to study its plants and animals.

Both KISR and KFAS also provided technical and financial support to the Kuwait science club, which aims to develop interest in scientific hobbies and provide the young with experience in the use of machinery and equipment in the club's workshops and laboratories.

In 1986 KFAS moved into its new headquarters with auditorium and lecture rooms and a library as well as offices, in a remarkable twelve-storey building in the city centre. The main lobby is dominated by a Foucault pendulum which rotates from west to east, 74.5 degrees every twenty-four hours, above a great slab of marble, and the open reception area is lit by a gigantic skylight and octagonal windows with crystallized glass which diffuse the fierce Kuwaiti sunlight. It has the atmosphere of a cathedral dedicated to science.

The Amir Shaikh Jaber al-Ahmad put forward his own suggestion for popularizing science in the Arab world, which was to translate into Arabic *Scientific American*, a magazine with a huge international circulation which already appears in French, German, Italian, Russian and Hungarian. Having secured the rights, KFAS formed a special company for the purpose and the first issue appeared in May 1986. Each issue has eight articles, of which seven are translations, while the eighth may be written originally in Arabic provided it is of a high enough standard.

One of the refreshing aspects of Kuwait is that the powerful and justified pride in the scientific achievements of the Arab/Islamic world in its Golden Age does nothing to prevent the knowledge that the Arabs as a whole have to make a supreme effort to catch up with the technical advances of the industrialized countries. In this field the Kuwait engineers' association is making an important contribution by compiling and publishing in eleven volumes a comprehensive Arabic dictionary of technical terms in engineering, technology and science which is exported to the other Arab states.

At the same time Kuwaitis have no doubt that the Arab and Islamic heritage still has much relevance to the present day. This is the principle behind the Islamic medicine centre. Not surprisingly, it is the view of the ministry of *awqaf* (Islamic endowments) and Islamic affairs. One of the projects it has sponsored is the compilation of a gigantic encyclopedia of Islamic law. This is the first of its kind in the Muslim world; previous attempts in Cairo and Damascus were started but came to nothing. A Syrian scholar, Dr Abdul Sattar Abu-Ghuddah, has been working on this colossal project for twenty years. Eight volumes out of twenty to twenty-five have been published so far and the encyclopedia should be completed by 1990. The difficulty which holds up the work is that it requires highly qualified experts in the field of jurisprudence who are extremely rare and are normally engaged in other full-time work. Dr Abu-Ghuddah explains that 'Islamic jurisprudence is basically the understanding of all the legal answers that face people from the sources of Islamic tradition.' But he adds that the interpretation in this encyclopedia is in accordance with the twentieth-century perspective, and great care has been taken in utilizing the most up-to-date classification methods. Eventually the plan is to translate the work into English, Swahili, Urdu and Turkish to make it available to nearly all the world's 800 million Sunni Muslims.

The outstanding manifestation of the Islamic heritage in Kuwait is both public and private. It is public because it is part of the country's National Museum; it is private because it is the collection of a member of the Sabah family – Shaikh Nasser Sabah al-Ahmed, the son of the foreign minister, and his wife, Shaikha Hussa Sabah al-Salem. It is an awesome delight. Cairo has a bigger collection of Egyptian works and Damascus of Syrian artefacts, but this is much the largest collection in the Arab world, covering the whole range of Islamic art from the Ummayads in the seventh century to the Moghuls in the twentieth century, and stands comparison with those in the British Museum, the Metropolitan, Louvre or the Hermitage. Any world tour by Islamic art-lovers now has to take in Kuwait. Shaikh Nasser and Shaikha Hussa are young and active and their collection is still growing. Gaps have to be filled but the collection is especially strong in the field of calligraphy, demonstrating the astonishing variety of its uses over the centuries.

A Nation of 'Nadwas'

T he Kuwaitis passionately enjoy discussion. No day passes – even at the height of the summer holiday season – without the holding of a *nadwa*, which may be translated as 'seminar' or 'symposium'. Sometimes there are two or three on the same day and their proceedings are reported extensively in the press. A *nadwa* may be sponsored by various bodies or institutions such as a bank, a newspaper, a professional association or one of Kuwait's many clubs (a club in Arabic is *nadi*, which has the same root as *nadwa*). The subject may be almost anything – cultural, political, social or economic. Examples taken at random during one week included the state of the fishing industry, the future of Arab theatre, conditions in the Israeli-occupied territories, the prospects for the bond market, air pollution from auto-mobiles and the history of the Arabs in Andalusia. If the subject does not concern Kuwait alone – and even if it does – there will always be a participant from elsewhere in the Arab world. Usually at least one of the speakers is a woman.

The Kuwaiti love of debate and the forceful expression of opinion has been reflected in parliament. Unfortunately it has not yet been possible to find a formula for a parliamentary system which is compatible with the effective government of the country. In the early 1970s the young university-trained technocrats who increasingly formed the executive branch of the government found the National Assembly both factional and disruptive. One of the problems was that division of the country into ten constituencies ensured that each of the different elements in Kuwaiti society – the merchants, the new middle class, the beduins and the Shia – gained control over one or more of them. The elected deputies then acted in parliament as representatives of the groups they came from and con-centrated on a narrow range of interests. It was only in the matter of acquiring control over the oil industry that the Assembly took a forward attitude. In this it was usually ahead of the government. But in other respects it constantly prevented the government from taking the actions it thought were necessary, while at times a conservative majority, which was the only majority the parliament could produce, took decisions which the government regarded as positively regressive.

Both the radical nationalist group in parliament and some leading university-educated technocrats believed that the solution was to allow the formation of political parties which might transcend sectarian differences, and a debate was sparked off on the subject in the national press. But the Amir and his family were resolutely opposed to the idea on the grounds that it would not alleviate but deepen the existing divisions in the Kuwaiti community, which was too small to afford them. There is little doubt that the majority of Kuwaitis agreed. When some outstanding and well-educated personalities formed a new grouping called the Liberal Democrats, which they deemed a political party but was intended to serve the interests of the nation as a whole rather than any one social group, they failed to come near to winning any seats in the 1975 elections.

The situation deteriorated to the point that, in August 1976, Shaikh Jaber al-Ahmad, the crown prince and prime minister, resigned with his cabinet declaring that it was no longer possible to carry on with the government. The Amir then suspended the National Assembly and the relevant articles in the constitution. He said he did so 'with a heart and soul full of sadness and pain, as conditions have deteriorated in our beloved country to an extent I have never imagined possible'. He said he was suspending parliament 'in order that freedom may continue to exist in our country with more steadfastness and stability, and in order that it may be enjoyed by all our people'.

The Amir said a committee of 'experienced and prominent citizens' would be set up to consider amending the constitution to remedy its defects and report to him and the Council of Ministers. The amended constitution would then be referred to the people either in a referendum or through a newly elected National Assembly within four years.

Although most Kuwaitis recognized the enormous defects of the National Assembly, there were many who regretted the suspension of parliamentary life. A statement put out by a group of professional and cultural associations claimed that the fact of Kuwait's democracy had given the country unique international prestige.

The government was as good as its word and parliamentary life was restored with elections to a new National Assembly in February 1981. Although the new Assembly was younger and better educated than its predecessors – the average age of the deputies was forty-three and over a third had university degrees – it still reflected the same social groups, and on this occasion it was dominated by the conservative beduin element. Representatives of the militantly Islamic Society for Social Reform also won five of the fifty seats. Despite the misgivings, the Assembly in many respects performed well as an increasingly effective organ of government at a time of acute difficulty and crisis which saw the shattering effect of the Suq al-Manakh crash in 1982, bomb outrages in Kuwait City in 1983, and the general menace of the unending Iraq–Iran war.

Fresh elections in February 1985 produced an Assembly which still had a conservative majority but in which an effective *de facto* opposition of radicals and independents increased in size and cohesion. However, soon after the election, relations within the Assembly began rapidly to deteriorate. Feeling the wind in their sails, deputies began to make life impossibly difficult for ministers with a deluge of questions and the mounting of highly personalized attacks. Several ministers came to regret that they had accepted office.

In March the crown prince and prime minister, Shaikh Saad al-Abdullah, returned to Kuwait after a prolonged absence to a huge popular welcome. It was known that he was deeply unhappy with the relations between his government and parliament but the Amir still held back from a dissolution. In May the minister of justice was forced to resign. Two other ministers tried to resign and, when their resignations were refused, they remained in the firing line. The deputies' attacks concentrated mainly on the government's limitations on their right to investigate and control financial policy. They sought to decide how the finance minister should remedy the consequences of the stock market crash and they insisted on the right, which was upheld by the constitutional court, to investigate and subpoena central bank officials. The education minister was under specific attack from the Islamic fundamentalists, who regarded him as excessively secular. The Assembly debates, which in the past had been generally good-humoured even when hard-hitting, became increasingly bitter.

The government/parliament crisis came to a head in June. The situation was already tense because of the Iranian occupation of the Faw peninsula a few miles from Kuwait's border. When four bombs exploded under an oil pipeline at Ahmadi, few doubted that agents of Iran were responsible. Deputies now launched a sharp attack on the oil minister, alleging he had been lax in security measures.

On 1 July the cabinet resigned on the same grounds that its predecessor had resigned ten years earlier – that it was impossible to carry on its work. Two days later the Amir dissolved the National Assembly and suspended indefinitely the articles in the constitution which stipulated that fresh elections had to be held within two months. In his speech to the nation he accused the deputies of obstruction but also warned against foreign-inspired subversion and sectarianism. His message was clear that such a state of affairs was far too dangerous to continue as it had been. As part of the clampdown, censorship was imposed on the press.

Any study of Kuwaiti society and its history showed that the situation was unlikely to remain frozen indefinitely. Some form of consultation, or *shura*, of the people by the ruler seemed certain to be revived, although it could be in a very different form. At least one senior member of the ruling family firmly believed that some form of elected assembly was needed because 'if you rely on appointed members they will end up by being even more radical and obstructive to prove that they are independent'. The first democratic experiment – or experiments – were far from useless. The elements that were good in them will not be forgotten, while their obvious defects will be remembered as a warning. The Amir had promised that the constitution would be retained and the Assembly reconvened when the time was right.

Meanwhile the *diwaniyahs* and the *nadwas*, which are their modern version, continued. Indeed, ministerial *diwaniyahs*, in which ministers invite those most affected by their decisions to question them in person, were deliberately revived.

Nothing will stop Kuwaitis from questioning and arguing, and it is therefore no surprise that the Kuwaiti press should have developed into one of the most lively and readable in the Arab world. With the sad demise of Beirut as main capital of the Arab press, Kuwait has taken its place in many respects.

Like so much else in Kuwait, the press has grown with great speed from tiny seeds over the past fifty years. The father of the Kuwait press was Abdul Aziz Rasheed, a man of great learning and piety with a love of science, who saw the press as an instrument of education. With some difficulty he began publishing a monthly magazine, *Al-Kuwait*, in 1928. It had to be printed in Cairo and the copies took several days to reach Kuwait overland. Few Kuwaitis were literate but copies of the magazine would be read out and discussed at the evening *diwaniyahs*. It lasted for only two years, when Rasheed left for Indonesia, where he published a series of Arabic magazines jointly with Younis Bahry, a prominent Iraqi journalist, until his death in 1937.

In the 1930s Kuwait had no papers or magazines, although the new cultural club and public library provided some imported magazines and

books and encouraged the habit of reading. This was a time when a few
Kuwaitis began going abroad – mainly to Cairo – for their higher education.
In 1945 a Kuwait House was founded in the Egyptian capital as a centre for
Kuwaiti students. With independence it was to become the embassy. Its
director was Abdul Aziz Hussein, later a minister of state, and now an elder
statesman and still adviser to the Amir. He founded a magazine, *Al-Baatha*,
(*The Mission*) which created an impression with its outspoken articles on a
wide range of political and cultural subjects. It made Cairenes aware of the
Kuwaiti presence.

From the time of the first publication of *Al-Kuwait* magazine, Kuwait
remained without a printing press for twenty years and everything had to
be printed abroad. The first press was installed by the government for its
own use in 1947, and the following year saw the appearance of the first
magazine to be printed in Kuwait – *Al-Kazima*. A new era had begun. One
estimate is that, in the following thirty years, a total of 178 daily
newspapers, weekly and monthly magazines and other periodicals arrived
on the scene. Many have disappeared, but in 1990 well over one hundred
survived. There are six Arabic daily newspapers and two published in
English (which carry pages in Indian languages).

In the early days, publishing a newspaper or magazine was an act of
dedication. Circulations were tiny because the rate of literacy was still low
and there was little advertising. Individuals or families financed the
publishing from their own pockets. After independence in 1961 the press
began to flourish and it was then that all the leading dailies were founded.
However, it was before independence – in 1959 – that what might be called
the flagship of the modern Kuwait press was launched. This was the
monthly (cultural, educational and scientific) magazine *Al-Arabi*, published
by the ministry of information. The first editor, Dr Ahmed Zaky, was a
scholarly Egyptian scientist, and on his death in 1976 he was succeeded by
another Egyptian, Ahmed Bahaeddine, one of the best known journalists in
the Arab world, and in 1985 by the first Kuwaiti editor Muhammad al-
Rumaihi, an outspokenly radical intellectual. With a format akin to that of
the *Reader's Digest*, although with a rather higher cultural level, *Al-Arabi*
soon acquired, and has since maintained, its reputation as the first
magazine of its kind to circulate throughout the Arab world. It has had to
overcome many difficulties to distribute in other Arab states. Some were
technical, such as the lack of foreign currency in many countries. But
authoritarian Arab regimes which controlled their own presses were also
suspicious of this new magazine from abroad, although it was non-political.
It was, after all, owned by the Kuwait government, even if the government

did not interfere in editorial policy. *Al-Arabi* gradually overcame this problem, partly because of its patently high quality and educational value, but also because Kuwait as a small country with no pretensions to being a regional power could not be regarded as a political threat. I recall that in the early 1960s *Al-Arabi* was often the only imported Arabic periodical on sale in Cairo, Damascus or Baghdad.

The new dailies and weeklies founded after independence were privately owned by wealthy Kuwaiti individuals or families. Initially, nearly all the expertise had to be provided by other Arabs, who were mostly Palestinians, Egyptian or Lebanese. Many remain, although the proportion of Kuwaiti journalists has steadily increased. Of the 600 members of the Kuwaiti journalists' association, 130 are Kuwaiti. Editorial opinion in the press covers a very wide spectrum, from Islamic fundamentalism to the borders of Marxism, but it is noticeable that nearly every newspaper or magazine allows substantial space to opposing views. Guest columns by non-Kuwaitis, whether Arabs or foreigners, are a common feature of all the daily newspapers. The strength of government control of the press has varied since independence. For long periods it has been virtually non-existent, in accordance with the article in the constitution which says that 'The freedom of the press and of publishing is guaranteed.' After the dissolution of the National Assembly in 1976, some curbs were imposed and some publications were suspended for short periods – usually because of intemperate criticisms of other Arab governments. The same happened after the second dissolution and suspension of part of the constitution ten years later, only this time the government's main concern was the overriding need for national unity in the face of internal subversion and the menace of the Gulf war. The country was close to facing a wartime emergency.

It is my own belief that the independence and vitality of the Kuwaiti press is now so well established, even after fewer than thirty years, that it will survive. It was significant that, on the eve of the Islamic summit meeting in Kuwait in January 1987, when the country was under the particular strain of direct Iranian threats, it was two Kuwaiti newspapers which carried lengthy interviews with President Assad and Colonel Qaddafy which dealt with a variety of highly sensitive issues. It is doubtful whether these interviews could have appeared in the press of any other Arab country (except in that of either the Syrian or Libyan leaders themselves).

Some Western diplomats and journalists tend to describe the Kuwaiti press as sensational, and it is true that the dailies occasionally publish speculation as fact. This is picked up by the international news agencies and

makes a headline on a dull day. But for obvious reasons these Westerners do
not see the rest of what the Kuwaiti press has to say. Taken as a whole, it is
neither strident nor unbalanced and its reporting of Kuwaiti affairs –
including the opinions expressed in the multitudinous *nadwas* – is
admirable. Occasionally it resorts to bitter personalized attacks, but in the
field of competitive sensationalism and bias it has nothing which remotely
compares with the British popular press at its worst – or indeed with some of
those which still lay claim to the title of 'quality' newspapers.

In 1977 the Kuwait national news agency, KUNA, was founded.
Transmitting in Arabic and English, it now has offices functioning in sixteen
world capitals. From Vienna it collates and transmits the English service of
the Federation of Arab News Agencies. Its reputation for independence and
accuracy is now well established. It has, however, been known to take risks.
During the Islamic conference in Kuwait in January 1987 it reported that
Mr Terry Waite had been seized in Beirut. No other source would confirm
the news for some days but eventually it turned out to be true. Was KUNA
following a hunch or had one of its well-informed correspondents made a
scoop? We shall never know.

At the end of the Second World War, the minister of social affairs and
labour was a remarkable man named Professor Hamad Issa al-Rajeeb. In
1947 he wrote in the Kuwaiti magazine *Al-Baatha*, published in Cairo, a
series of articles on the need for theatre in Kuwait, deploring the fact that
there was no stage in the country. In the 1930s and 1940s plays were
occasionally performed in schools but they never came out from behind the
school walls. Professor al-Rajeeb said that he was aware that many people
thought that the theatre had no value or was contrary to the Arab/Islamic
tradition but he vigorously disagreed; it was an essential vehicle for
education and culture and a means for tackling social problems as well as a
source of entertainment. He pointed out that Egypt helped to subsidize its
own theatre and a drama school.

From this small beginning the Kuwaiti theatre grew to become one of the
best in the Arab world, rivalling those of Cairo and Damascus. In the words
of a prominent Iraqi poet, with whom in 1986 I attended the performance of
a new play by a young Kuwaiti author, it is also 'the most courageous'. In
1986 a Kuwaiti group won the Arab theatre prize in Baghdad with their
play *Hamdallah*.

If Professor al-Rajeeb gave the first impetus to the movement, it was
Muhammad al-Nashny, as dramatist, director and actor, who was the
father of the Kuwaiti theatre. His career lasted some forty-five years until his
death in 1984. Against initial indifference and lack of official cooperation, he

brought the theatre out of the schools to the general public. He founded two theatre companies and established a drama school. He soon found enthusiastic followers. Some Egyptian actors and directors were brought in. The Kuwaiti public took easily to the theatre both for its spectacle and the social comment and satire it provided. Virtually every play performed in Kuwait offers a mixture of this kind.

One play by a young Kuwaiti dramatist was an intricate blend of fantasy, tragedy and comedy. It had strong echoes of Brecht and Weiss but its references to characters in Arab history and literature gave it a totally Arab flavour. Since it was spoken in a mixture of classical Arabic and Kuwaiti colloquial, it would be impossible to translate. The audience was delighted.

This I suppose was *avant garde*, although much of the audience looked like the equivalent of those who in London would be attending *The Mousetrap*. Productions in the popular theatre in Kuwait are akin to the productions of Joan Littlewood. Popular songs are sung, there is much extemporization and the stage often appears to be in chaos. But the most popular performances have a sharp satirical bite. On a visit in 1980 I watched with astonishment on television a beautiful young Kuwaiti woman who had her own theatre troupe in a series of sketches on such subjects as drunkenness, the problems of bureaucracy and of Kuwaitis who marry foreigners. At the end of each sketch she would come before the curtain and discuss it with the audience. Kuwait now has a number of excellent actors of both sexes but perhaps the most outstanding – and certainly the one who is best known outside Kuwait – is Abdul Hussein Abdul Rida. Like Britain's Sir Alec Guinness, he brings to life an extraordinary range of characters. In collaboration with an Egyptian writer, he has created a series of satirical plays in which he directs and plays the lead, and which through video have become famous throughout the Arab world. The best-known, *Bye Bye London*, is about the behaviour of Arabs in Britain. *Fursan al-Manakh* (*Knights of al-Manakh*) is a wicked satire on the greed and naiveté which led to the stock market crash. The latest is a frontal assault on the current state of the Arab world entitled *Bye Bye Arabs*.

As might be expected, the theatre interrelates with television, and Abdul Rida has produced several serials. Some Kuwaiti soap operas have become extremely popular and, although they are usually performed in the Kuwaiti dialect, they have been shown with success as far away as Tunisia. I watched a new one in rehearsal which concerned two sisters from a modest background who, having suddenly become rich through the sale of some land to the government, had decided to set up their own estate agency.

Their first attempts to wear what they thought was suitable dress for
modern businesswomen were disastrous but they were learning their
profession rapidly and standing up to predatory clients and relations. The
fact that they employed the husband of one of the sisters to manage their
public relations says something about the position of women in Kuwaiti
society.

The purely entertainment programmes on television of songs and dances
are unlikely to be to Western taste, and there is no reason why they should
be. Rows of ravishingly beautiful girls in brilliant enveloping costumes sing
in unison or move in stately procession. Occasionally the young men
attempt a more ambitious choreography. Soloists sing at great length about
romantic love and sometimes about patriotism. A few have real talent and
sincerity, and in time a Westerner can learn to distinguish these in Arab
singers. There are others who have neither. There is one very young girl –
Kuwait's answer to Shirley Temple – who must be avoided at any cost.

Some of the material on both the television channels is imported from
both the Arab world and the West. Egypt is a major source of films and
television serials but there is an increasing quantity from other Arab
countries such as Jordan, Algeria and Iraq, while there are frequent
American films and British documentaries. Kuwait has a small but
flourishing film industry of its own. Khalid Siddiqi's *Bas ya Bahr* (translated
as *The Cruel Sea*) and his *Wedding of Zein*, a film of the novella by the noted
Sudanese writer Tayeb Salih, have achieved recognition beyond the Arab
countries and recently the Kuwaiti industry seems to have received a new
impetus. However, as far as the Kuwaiti theatre and television drama are
concerned, there is a feeling that, after a great flowering in the late 1960s
and 1970s, they are passing through a recession. One fear that is sometimes
expressed is that, while drama in schools' and children's theatre are
flourishing, plays for adults are becoming too bland.

The government has given support. In 1973 it founded a Higher Institute
of Dramatic Arts and subsidizes the five individual theatre companies. The
magnificent conference centre which was built for the Islamic summit
meeting in January 1987 has a large auditorium which is to become a
national theatre. But directors and actors complain this is not nearly
enough. As one told me, it is a small proportion of what is provided for sport.
In a recent interview Abdul Hussein Abdul Rida appealed to the governments of all the Arab Gulf states, saying that without government support
'the theatre movement will collapse', although he praised what the Saudi
Arabian and Qatari governments as well as the Kuwaiti government had
done in the past. The appeal sounds familiar to anyone from the West – not

least from Britain – but this does not mean it is not well founded. It would be a tragic loss for Kuwait's cultural life if the theatre were to enter a permanent decline.

Kuwaiti television is used to replay the favourite national pastime of the *nadwa*. The many visitors to Kuwait who are outstanding figures in Arab political, religious, academic or cultural life are subjected to interviews which are usually searching and expertly conducted. Kuwait television sometimes makes its own documentaries. One series of special interest was of dramatized versions of real crimes followed by a discussion between a judge, a police officer and a criminologist. In one, a respectable Kuwaiti father lost heavily through gambling and, when his appeals to his wealthy brother for help for his destitute family were refused, he turned in desperation to attempted bank robbery and was caught. In the discussion which followed, the brother was blamed almost as much as the culprit.

Kuwait radio has expanded in pace with Kuwaiti society. In 1951 it first went on the air for two hours a day; now a total of sixty-two hours are transmitted each day on eight channels, broadcasting in English, French, Persian and Urdu, as well as Arabic. Correspondence received by the Persian service shows that it has a substantial audience in Iran; Radio Tehran's Arabic broadcasts are not a one-way channel of influence. Another special channel of news, commentaries, serials and music is beamed to the Kuwaiti and other Arab communities living in Europe.

Radio is another lovely medium for the *nadwa* in a different form. Phone-in programmes are popular and it is possible to hear the expression of some startling opinions. Although television and radio are state monopolies, they are both able and willing to broadcast a wide range of views.

In August 1988 the ending of hostilities in the Iraq–Iran war which had been one of the main justifications for the closure of parliament and the imposition of press censorship, inevitably began to revive pressure for the restoration of democratic life and the removal of censorship.

It would be fanciful to compare the situation with that in Eastern Europe. Kuwaiti citizens enjoy incomparably more political and human rights than those living under the former communist regimes. The leaders of the pro-democracy movement in Kuwait – and indeed the entire Kuwaiti electorate – are educated, affluent and middle-class and none was in prison for actively seeking democracy. It was said that their movement was the first of its kind to be organized on the car telephone. Yet the electrifying news from Europe during the autumn and winter of 1989/90 made them more persistent and enthusiastic in their demands.

The movement gathered strength towards the end of 1989 at a series of *diwaniyahs* held in the private houses of individuals, many of them former members of the National Assembly. A group of 50 citizens organized a petition asking for the recall of the Assembly which obtained 25,000 signatories – the equivalent of 40 per cent of the electorate. But the Amir and the Crown Prince/Prime Minister refused to be rushed. The government issued stern warnings that the *diwaniyahs* should not be expanded into substitute parliaments. The Amir appealed for calm in a speech to the nation saying, 'Let us always remember that we are members of the same tiny community which cannot tolerate dissension . . . and where it is easy to come to terms given good intentions and open-mindedness.' The Crown Prince promised that the government would sound out public opinion, saying that the problems of the old Assembly required some new form of democracy but the principle of public political participation was not in question.

However, in the waiting for the dialogue between the government and the petitioners to begin, the public agitation continued in the form of rallies held at the homes of former deputies in Kuwait City. These were generally peaceful but at one on 22 January 1990 tough police action led to a few injuries and the arrest of a handful of people who were held in custody for a few days.

The situation calmed when the Crown Prince agreed to meet a series of delegations of deputies. The problem remained that the Amir and Crown Prince still believed that there must be changes in the form and structure of Kuwait's parliamentary democracy, while the deputies mostly insisted on a return to the constitution and the pre-1986 system. The Crown Prince suggested that negotiations to achieve a compromise would take a long time and the deputies replied that if the delay was too long they would renew their agitation. But in the light of Kuwait's history the hopes that a compromise would be found were realistic.

The Amir, after consultation with the Crown Prince, decided to act to create his own compromise. He told the nation on 22 April 1990 that after taking into account all the opinions expressed by a wide spectrum of Kuwaiti society he had decided that a provisional National Assembly would be established with 75 members of whom 50 would be elected by secret ballot while the remaining 25 would be appointed 'on the basis of qualifications and experience'. During the four years of its mandate the Assembly's main task would be to 'study the reasons for the difficulties that arose between the executive and legislative branches of the government with a view to finding ways of avoiding them in the future.' But the

Assembly would also have powers to question ministers on government policy and to debate the budget before it was promulgated. Elections were to be held on 10 June.

The immediate reaction of many of the former deputies was to claim that the Amir was using a device to alter the parliamentary system as stipulated in the constitution. In fact what the Amir was doing was to place the onus for reforming the system on the members of the provisional Assembly. At the same time he was making clear that Kuwait had no intention of abandoning the principle of elected representative institutions which still makes the country unique among the Arab Gulf states.

Facing the Future

On a warm and sunny afternoon in late March 1986, Shaikh Saad Abdallah al-Salem al-Sabah, Kuwait's crown prince and prime minister, returned to his country after several months' absence. Some of the skyscrapers and flyovers in the gleaming modern city, choked by nearly one million vehicles, had not been there when he left. Yet the type of welcome he received from the Kuwaitis emphasized that this was no depersonalized metropolis but still a small and tightly knit community. As he stood for several hours in a receiving line, it seemed as if at least a third of Kuwait's male population had turned out to greet him. He seemed to know them all personally, and in return they were aware of the exact nature of the relationship. Those who were closest kissed him on both cheeks, some kissed him on the forehead, while others shook hands. A few small children were held up to be embraced.

On the following day, the crown prince drove out northwards to review Kuwait's advanced military positions near the Iraqi border. The Kuwaiti armed forces are small but well equipped. Conscription for eighteen months' service, which was introduced in 1978, has swelled the numbers to about 12,500, and even young diplomats serving abroad have to return annually as reservists for a month.

This was an anxious time. The Iranians had recently occupied the Faw peninsula. Heavy artillery barrages could often be heard and seen across the narrow waters of the Gulf at night. However, Kuwaitis were not living on the edge of their nerves or bent over their radio sets to hear the news, as some Western newspapers were describing them. I found that, after watching some extraordinary film on Iraqi television of fighting in Fao and Kurdistan, Kuwaiti friends had turned to the other Channel to watch a Hollywood comedy in which Donald O'Connor found himself by mistake in a women's unit of the US army.

Possibly this was escapism. Everyone in Kuwait was aware that it was the eye of the great storm in the Gulf. Iran regarded Kuwait as the ally of Iraq which it could most easily intimidate. In the winter of 1986–87 ships bound to and from Kuwait were being increasingly attacked by the Iranians who sometimes seized their cargoes on the ground that they were destined for Iraq.

The Kuwaiti Government approached both the USSR and US to help meet the threat which was intensified by Iran's installation of Chinese-made surface-to-surface Silkworm missile batteries within range of Kuwaiti territory. The first American response was to suggest a convoy system to which Britain and France would contribute warships, but the Kuwaitis were reluctant to accept as this would seem to tie Kuwait too closely to the West and contravene its policy of non-alignment with either of the superpowers. After some delay the Soviet Union said it would lease three Russian tankers to Kuwait and thereby entitle part of Kuwait's oil exports to Soviet naval protection.

The Soviet offer and Kuwait's acceptance stimulated the United States into action. It now proposed the establishment of a US-registered holding company to which ownership of 11 of Kuwait's tankers would be transferred. The US would then use its navy to protect tankers flying the US flag. This reflagging of Kuwaiti tankers with the Stars and Stripes and the leasing of Soviet tankers avoided any direct military commitment to either of the superpowers. The Kuwaitis declared that the foreign escorting warships would not be allowed into Kuwaiti territorial waters where Kuwait would be responsible for their protection.

Iran's Islamic Republic did not accept that Kuwait had remained non-aligned and launched a torrent of abuse, accusing the Kuwaitis of subservience to the great powers, declaring that Kuwait would 'pay the price' for its action and exhorting 'Kuwaiti Muslims' to teach their government a lesson. Some of Kuwait's Gulf partners, such as the United Arab Emirates and Oman, were uneasy at what they saw as the widening of the war, but the Kuwaitis were undeterred because they were convinced they had no alternative. As the Foreign Minister later remarked: 'We did not go into reflagging because we wanted to internationalize the conflict but because oil production was cut by 40 to 50 per cent.'

Initially there were doubts about the steadfastness of the new US policy in the Gulf represented by the decision to reflag and protect the Kuwaiti tankers. While it obviously showed Washington's desire to restore US credibility with the moderate Arab Gulf states following the Irangate revelations and at the same time to prevent the Soviet Union from playing the major superpower role in the Gulf, doubts were raised by some US

Congressmen about the extent of the commitment and its cost. Some of them were alarmed by the apparent US tilt towards the Arabs and its consequences for Israel. One prominent New York columnist launched an extraordinary attack on the Amir of Kuwait, whom he accused of being a Middle East version of Machiavelli who was manipulating the US for his own purposes while showing no real sympathy for Western views on such matters as the price of oil or Afghanistan. On the other hand, there were US Senators such as Warner and Glenn who made clear their belief that a pre-emptive strike was likely to be necessary as soon as the Iranians made their Silkworm missiles operational.

Admiral Crowe, chairman of the US chiefs of staff, took the more measured view that although the US could not rule out Iran escalating the war there were signs that it was acting with caution. His judgement proved to be correct. In spite of blood-curdling threats from the Iranian leadership of retribution against the Great Satan for its intervention in the Gulf, the Iranians avoided providing justification for a full-scale US military strike against the Iranian mainland. They laid mines which holed both a US warship and a US-owned tanker but denied responsibility even when caught red-handed and proclaimed that their navy was 'selflessly' clearing all the mines from the Strait of Hormuz. When the Iranians succeeded on 16 October 1987 in hitting a US tanker in Kuwaiti waters with a Silkworm missile the US was forced to respond, although the ship's protection, according to Kuwait's own view, was Kuwait's responsibility. Three days later four destroyers from the growing US navy in the Gulf destroyed two inactive Iranian oil-rigs in the Central Gulf which the US claimed had been used to coordinate Iranian mine-laying activities. Another three days passed and another Iranian Silkworm missile fired from the occupied Faw peninsula partially destroyed Kuwait's Sea Island oil terminal.

This was the most serious direct Iranian assault on Kuwait until that time. The Kuwaitis not only set about speedily repairing the terminal but launched a programme to strengthen their defences by the purchase of their own new missiles from the West. However, it was significant that despite their violent rhetoric the Iranians were still avoiding the kind of action which would bring them into a full-scale confrontation with the United States. Iranian and American spokesmen both made it clear that, at least for the time being, the duel was over and honour had been satisfied.

Kuwait had some reasons for satisfaction. With considerable skill it was pursuing a course which emphasized that the country was still non-aligned and uncommitted to the US camp but at the same time did not provoke excessive resentment or charges of ingratitude from the US

Congress or the American public. These were generally relieved that President Reagan's policy in the Gulf was proving modestly successful after an earlier series of disastrous setbacks in the Middle East. At the same time the catastrophe caused by the rioting of Iranian pilgrims during the Islamic Pilgrimage season in August had consolidated opinion in the Arab and Islamic worlds against Iran and in Kuwait's favour. This was reflected in the resolutions of the Arab summit meeting in Amman in November 1987 which condemned Iran for continuing the war and expressed solidarity with Kuwait.

Kuwait's position still remained sensitive and dangerous. A stoical calm was required. There could be no question of Kuwait abandoning its support for Iraq in the war which has wholly transcended disagreements with Baghdad over demarcation of parts of the border between the two countries. This meant that Kuwait accepted that it would continue to be a prime target for Iranian enmity. But it also meant that Kuwait fervently hoped for the war to end through compromise. All Arab and Islamic attempts at mediation having failed because Iran regarded them as biassed in Iraq's favour, Kuwait looked to the alternative of resolute international action. The unanimous UN Security Council resolution No. 598 of 20 July 1987 seemed to offer some hope of this but the essential degree of great power cooperation to make it effective was still lacking. On the eve of the Reagen–Gorbachev summit meeting in Washington in December 1987 Iran launched another Silkworm missile at Kuwait. It missed its target and fell into the sea but everyone in Kuwait assumed that it was a characteristically defiant Iranian gesture to the two superpowers.

There are several reasons why Kuwait kept its nerve. One was a simple belief that the Iranians would not invade Kuwaiti territory and so inevitably internationalize the war. This was reinforced by the fact that, since 1981, Kuwait has been part of the Gulf Cooperation Council – the grouping of six Arab Gulf states which is moving gradually but steadily towards a common market and a form of federation. The headquarters of the GCC are in Riyadh and the secretary-general, Abdallah Bishara, is a dynamic and highly experienced Kuwaiti diplomat. The integration of the armed forces of the GCC states into a military organization which would be capable of undertaking the defence of the six states against all external threats is still an objective that lies some way in the future, although there has been good progress towards creating a coordinated air defence network based in Saudi Arabia. For the time being, the ultimate sanction to prevent the full blockade of shipping in the Gulf had to be the threat of intervention of the great powers and the full internationalization of the war. Increasing political integration with the five other Arab Gulf states undoubtedly adds to Kuwait's sense of security.

The main factor behind Kuwait's calmness and steadfastness in the front line must remain its inner self-confidence and the stability of its society. These have been severely tested by the series of bombings in 1983, and the subsequent terrorist acts which were primarily aimed at forcing Kuwait to release the seventeen Muslim fundamentalists who had been charged and convicted for the first attacks. Almost alone among states in the world, Kuwait has not only said it will refuse to bargain with any terrorist organization to secure protection but has also stood by its word. When in December 1984 a Kuwaiti airliner was hijacked by four Arab terrorists and taken to Tehran, the Kuwaitis refused to enter into any negotiations with the hijackers, despite the number of Kuwaiti citizens on board. This was not an easy decision to make when the families of virtually every Kuwaiti citizen are known to at least some members of the government. But there seems to have been no hesitation. In the same way, Kuwait consistently refused requests by the Archbishop of Canterbury's emissary Terry Waite to visit Kuwait to discuss the demands of the terrorists holding hostages in Lebanon who wanted to bargain for the release of the prisoners in Kuwait. The Kuwaiti government would not acknowledge that there was any connection between Kuwait's prisoners and hostages in Lebanon. To some, the attitude seemed harsh but it has since been amply justified, for the inescapable consequence of bargaining with kidnappers seems to be more kidnapping.

An important element in Kuwait's evident *sang froid* is the grave unflappability of the present Amir. A man who prefers to live very modestly, the Amir, to the astonishment of some of his Western visitors, likes to don very ordinary clothes and go shopping incognito in the *suq*. He is someone with whom the Kuwaiti-in-the-street can identify. On 25 May 1985 a suicide bomber drove a vehicle into his motorcade. Although among the injured, he at once appeared on television to reassure the public. Two months later two bomb explosions in seaside cafés killed nine and injured more than eighty but the city remained calm.

Kuwait cannot take its national unity for granted. Some two-thirds of the inhabitants of the country are not Kuwaiti and a minority of these may have no respect for the Kuwaiti state; but, beyond this, it cannot assume the loyalty of all its own citizens. On 1 February 1987 the minister of the interior announced the names of a dozen young Kuwaitis whom he accused of responsibility for recent bombings and attacks on oil installations. Previously arrested terrorists had been non-Kuwaitis – mostly Iraqi Shiites.

Some of these had the names of celebrated Kuwaiti families who were of Iranian origin but long established in Kuwait. A few of the heads of these families took out advertisements in the press to affirm their loyalty and deny any connection with the young fanatics.

The Kuwaiti public was patently upset by the event. However, as the days passed, it was apparent that the great majority of the 25 per cent of Kuwaitis who are Shiite and/or of Iranian origin had no sympathy with such desperate acts. If some of them grumble and allege that they do not have full equality with Kuwait Sunnis in every respect, they are loyal to the Kuwaiti state and certainly have no wish to be forcibly absorbed into a Greater Islamic Republic of Iran.

The tension in Kuwait rose inexorably. In April 1988 there was a new hijacking of a Kuwaiti airliner by Shiite militants demanding the release of the 17 convicted saboteurs in a Kuwaiti jail. The hijackers forced the plane to fly to Mashad in Iran where they held 30 Kuwaiti hostages including one male and two female members of the al-Sabah ruling family. But the Kuwait government stood by its principle of refusing to respond to such blackmail. After 16 days the affair ended in Algiers. The hijackers were allowed to escape but the hostages returned to an emotional and popular welcome in Kuwait.

In the early summer there were more bombing and sabotage incidents in Kuwait. The ceasefire in the Iraq–Iran war in August 1988 was the cause of restrained joy and intense relief. In spite of Iraq's military victories in the early summer, Ayatollah Khomeini's sudden acceptance of UN Resolution 598 for a ceasefire (a decision he described as 'more deadly than taking poison') came as a surprise.

The country's outlook was transformed. During the eight years of war all planning for the future had been subordinated to security. Conscious of the fact that while Kuwait owns some 10 per cent of the world's oil reserves it accounts for only just over 2 per cent of global output Kuwait began in 1989 to push for an increase in its OPEC quota of 5.61 per cent or 1.15 million barrels per day out of a total of 22.1 million barrels per day, and received grudging acceptance of a rise to 1.5 million barrels per day or about 6.75 per cent of the OPEC total at the OPEC summit meeting in November 1989. However, for the time being the increase was academic since Kuwait had for some time been producing at well above its quota, with an output verging on 2 million barrels per day – on the ground that with oil prices well above the OPEC reference price of $18 per barrel, overproduction was permissible.

The increase of revenues of more than 50 per cent in the first half of 1989 compared with the first half of 1988 enabled the government to increase public spending, raise wages and salaries and launch various domestic construction projects which had been delayed by the war and recession. The mood of the private sector became noticeably more buoyant. At the same time, as part of an economic reform package announced in December 1989, the government was able to clear up most of the remnants of the 1982 Suq al-Manakh crash by forgiving all 'small' debtors (defined as those with debts up to 250,000 Kuwaiti dinars or $825,000) a large part of their bank debt.

Kuwait's economic prospects in the 1990s are encouraging and stimulating. They cannot, however, be predicted with any certainty. While most Kuwaitis are convinced that the decade will see both a gradual hardening of oil prices and swing back to the Gulf as the world's most important oil-producing region, experience shows that predictions of the world oil market are as hazardous as predicting weather trends in the British Isles. The world's most experienced oil analysts are deeply divided on the subject. Nevertheless, the size of Kuwait's oil reserves in relation to its population and the scale of its overseas investments ensure that in any circumstances the small maritime desert Emirate will remain an economic power of world importance.

The political outlook in the 1990s, while also greatly improved by the ending of the war, is also uncertain. Until the Gulf ceasefire is transformed into a permanent peace agreement, of which there was little prospect in 1990, uneasiness will prevail. The appeal of Khomeinism to Kuwaiti Shiites has declined but not disappeared. Kuwait may no longer be in the eye of the storm but, surrounded by larger and more powerful neighbours whose own relationships are tense, Kuwait can never be immune to turbulence in the region. Similarly, it has to be conscious of the fact that these neighbours are watching with concern, sometimes mixed with apprehension, Kuwait's internal developments and its experiments in parliamentary democracy. The restoration of Kuwaiti press freedom, already partially achieved, will increase the importance of Kuwait's example.

One thing seems certain: Kuwait will not abandon its independent and non-aligned foreign policy or its attempts to mediate in matters affecting fellow Arabs or Muslims. It was wholly typical that when Kuwait signed an agreement in August 1988 to buy $1.9 million worth of US aircraft and missiles it had only recently agreed to buy a consignment of Soviet armoured personnel carriers. When the commander in chief of the US Central Command visited Kuwait in October 1989 and publicly pledged US military support for Kuwait against outside attack his arrival nearly coincided with that of President Ortega of Nicaragua. At the same time, the Kuwait government was attempting to mediate between Senegal and Mauritania, which had come to the brink of war over a border dispute, and played an active role in the question of the maltreatment of ethnic Turks in Bulgaria, eventually persuading both Turkey and Bulgaria to send delegations to Kuwait to discuss the matter.

The fact that Kuwait seems set to become increasingly integrated into the political, military and economic structures of the Gulf Corporation Council, which are becoming better established each year, does not mean that Kuwait's specific character is likely to become diluted. On the contrary, it is certain that the atmosphere will remain subtly but unmistakably different from that in Riyadh, Bahrain or Muscat. The country will remain committed to its belief in strict neutrality between the great powers. It would be surprising if it does not undertake some new experiment in political institutions. Kuwaitis will maintain their own way of looking at things.

Nevertheless, the six members of the GCC have much in common in the structure of their societies and their outlook on the world. This is the basis of the success of their efforts to move closer to each other. Each of them has to face the same problems of how to modernize rapidly without damage to their inherited identity and how to reduce their dependence on a limited national resource.

Oil was discovered first in Bahrain but in relatively small quantities. Huge reserves were found in Saudi Arabia and Kuwait at about the same time – just before the Second World War – but, in contrast to Kuwait, the vast kingdom of Saudi Arabia had to make use of all its revenues in order to create a modern economic and social infrastructure. Kuwait was the first of the oil city-states with a surplus which could be loaned to needier countries or invested for the future. This was reflected in the creation of the Kuwait Investment Office in London in 1958 and the Kuwait Arab Development Fund in 1961.

The trend towards modernization has powerfully affected Kuwait for some forty years. But modernization should not be simply equated with Westernization or secularism. As always in the Middle East, the real situation is much more complex. In many respects, '*plus le Koweit change, plus c'est la même chose*'. With the first rush of affluence in the 1950s every Kuwaiti who could afford it left the country during the savage summer heat. It seemed to me at the time that Kuwait would in the future be actively deserted during July and August. However, this has not happened. Ubiquitous air-conditioning and television and multiplying recreation and entertainment facilities have made life much more tolerable. Sailing marines, beach clubs, holiday resorts on Failaka Island and near the Saudi Arabian border have been built. There is an entertainment city resembling Disneyland and an immensely popular skating rink. The wealthiest Kuwaitis may have their own homes in Marbella, Geneva or London, where they will spend part of the summer, but others of more modest means now often say that they prefer the relaxed atmosphere of Kuwait to the hurly-burly of a European hotel in high summer. Beach chalets provide privacy and calm. Urban life for many generations has not destroyed Kuwaitis' attraction to the freedom of the desert. In fact the nostalgia is growing, and not only among the beduin elements in the population. At weekends and during school holidays the landscape outside Kuwait City is dotted with private tents. Inside there are air-conditioning units, freezers and video machines, but the nearest neighbour is a quarter of a mile away and the noise of the city cannot be heard.

When the old Kuwait City was swept away in the 1960s, new suburbs of villas with gardens, often with bizarre individual architecture, spread in the desert. In the city centre nearly all the old one- and two-storey buildings gave way to new blocks of increasing height. Skyscraper hotels and offices were acceptable but high-rise apartments were not a success. Now a huge project is under way in south Kuwait to erect a replica of the residential areas of old Kuwait on a 2 million square metre site with spacious houses built round cool interior courtyards and an old-style *suq* serving the community. Part of the scheme is to attract contemporary Kuwaiti artists to occupy some of the houses.

This is a striking example of Kuwait's tendency to blend the old with the new. Sculpture and painting – the 'formative arts' as they are called, because creation is an attribute only of God – are not in the Arab/Islamic tradition. But, starting in a modest way in schools some thirty years ago, the government has encouraged a modern art movement in the country, providing studio facilities, staging exhibitions, publishing books of artists' work and helping them to exhibit abroad and commissioning works of sculpture for public places. A Kuwait biennial exhibition for Arab formative artists is now a well-established event. State sponsorship would be useless if the movement was unable to set down roots of its own but there is now clear evidence that this is happening. Some private art galleries are being established in Kuwait.

The encouragement of new art combines with the promotion of Kuwait's own cultural heritage. An annual 'Day of the Sea' in March com-memorates Kuwait's roots in pearling and fishing and huge crowds throng the beaches. Celebrations of traditional dancing and music are vastly popular, but few Kuwaitis would see anything strange in returning home to watch a Western film on television. At a deeper level I have tried to show in how many different ways – through its cultural and financial institutions, its research institutes and museums, and the unending discussions of the *nadwas* – Kuwait is attempting to apply traditional Islamic values to the modern world.

Nothing exemplifies the apparent paradox of Kuwait's progressive conservatism more than the position of women. In relation to the simple certainties of a Western feminist, Kuwaiti women have a long way to go. Yet, as we have seen, they have experienced a much more revolutionary social change than the men in the past forty years. From being virtually uneducated, they now have a higher proportion of university degrees (with better levels) than the males. They play an active role in public life as senior civil servants, heads of university departments, doctors and lawyers; they even hold their own with men in the theatre. For me perhaps the most startling demonstration of emancipation was the brilliant twenty-three-year-old woman doctor who was researching into AIDS. Any reasonable observer would admit that the cause for surprise is not that women should have been denied the vote to the National Assembly but that so many Kuwaiti men as well as women should have demanded it. Only 25 out of the 200 active members of the lawyers' association are women; an old Kuwaiti hand would be astonished that there were so many.

However, the crucial aspect is the self-confidence of Kuwaiti women. This is relevant because of the recent growth of Islamic feelings, or what is more properly called Islamic reassertion, in the region. Will this set back the trend towards female emancipation? Here the greatest caution is required for any Western observer. The first point to be noted is that even militant Kuwaiti feminists – and they are not rare – do not regard their views as incompatible with Islam. The young girls who have chosen to wear modern Islamic dress covering all but their face and hands have not done so because they want to retire to the harem. On the contrary, they want to take part in public life without having to put up with male harassment. When working with males who are not their husbands, they want their sex to be ignored, which is presumably the ideal of the Western feminist.

It is true that in neighbouring Iran, where women played an important and active role in the Islamic Revolution, the result has been to deprive them of some of their positions in public life such as in law or industry. But the position in Kuwait is very different. Kuwaiti women as a whole are much better educated than their Iranian sisters, and even the most pious among their leaders would not wish to see them confined to their homes. They are well able to stand up to those militantly Islamic males who would like this to happen. I recall with delight watching a televised *nadwa* in which a distinguished Kuwaiti regretted the disappearance of the simple inward-looking family life in the old Kuwaiti homes of a generation ago. He was briskly demolished by a young professional mother, who pointed out that such nostalgia was all very well for the men but modern amenities not only relieved her of drudgery but enabled her to be a much better mother to her children and more capable of helping with their education. All this was in addition to her contribution to the progress of Kuwait through her professional work.

On 2 February 1987 Shaikh Jaber al-Ahmad addressed his people on television. He spoke with justifiable pride of Kuwait's success in arranging, in the face of considerable doubts and opposition, the summit meeting of forty-five Muslim or partly Muslim nations which had just taken place. He concluded by saying, 'Nations are not only measured by the size of their population or the extent of their territory but by their people's capacity for achievement.' He also said that 'a rightly guided society is one which finds a just balance between constraint and consent and which neither lets the criminal to go unpunished nor the innocent bear the blame for others'.

I hope that, in this personal view of a country for which I have developed an affectionate esteem over thirty years, I have provided some reasons why I regard the Amir's pride, characteristically modest and dignified in its expression, to be justifiable. Kuwait has the closest affinities with its fellow members of the Gulf Cooperation Council, and in no way regards itself as an exceptional or outlandish member of the wider communities of the Arab and Islamic worlds. But it does have a powerful individual personality. In my view, one of the most valuable strands in this personality is the combination of vigorous and outspoken individualism with respect for the law, enabling the government, in the Amir's words, to combine constraint with consent. That the expression of this balance through one form of parliamentary democracy has been suspended is largely due to the peculiarly difficult and dangerous circumstances in which Kuwait finds itself today. It is wholly characteristic that a new form of representative government has been created and put into effect.

The truth is that Kuwait has been an open society throughout the two centuries of its existence, even when it appeared as a remote backwater to most of the outside world. It never withdrew into itself like other parts of Arabia, such as Yemen, Najd or Oman, have done in recent times. Kuwait was on great caravan routes and its people traded and travelled. Moreover, the groups in its society shared political power. Its rulers were sometimes authoritarian but they were never absolute; the Sabah family has been *primus inter pares* and has not sought for more.

When I told an experienced British Arabist friend I was going to write this book, he asked, 'How will you manage to deal with the Suq al-Manakh crash? Surely the Kuwaitis will be extremely sensitive.' Shortly afterwards I was making my first visit to the headquarters of KFAS, the Kuwait Fund for the Advancement of Sciences, which was the brainchild of the Amir. Dr Ali Shemlan, the director-general, described the fund's various annual prizes, including the one for the best book on Kuwait. 'This year,' he said, 'the prize may well go to a book on the stock market crisis by a young Kuwaiti economist.' I asked for a copy and discovered that it was a sharp indictment not only of the actions which led to the crash but of most of the government's economic policies over the past decade. Liberalism of this kind testifies to an inner self-confidence which is surely a matchless asset.

Index